Burgers in Blackface

Forerunners: Ideas First

Short books of thought-in-process scholarship, where intense analysis, questioning, and speculation take the lead

FROM THE UNIVERSITY OF MINNESOTA PRESS

Kelly Oliver
Carceral Humanitarianism: Logics of Refugee Detention

P. David Marshall
The Celebrity Persona Pandemic

Davide Panagia
Ten Theses for an Aesthetics of Politics

David Golumbia
The Politics of Bitcoin: Software as Right-Wing Extremism

Sohail Daulatzai
Fifty Years of *The Battle of Algiers*: Past as Prologue

Gary Hall
The Uberfication of the University

Mark Jarzombek
Digital Stockholm Syndrome in the Post-Ontological Age

N. Adriana Knouf
How Noise Matters to Finance

Andrew Culp
Dark Deleuze

Akira Mizuta Lippit
Cinema without Reflection: Jacques Derrida's Echopoiesis and Narcissism Adrift

Sharon Sliwinski
Mandela's Dark Years: A Political Theory of Dreaming

Grant Farred
Martin Heidegger Saved My Life

Ian Bogost
The Geek's Chihuahua: Living with Apple

Shannon Mattern
Deep Mapping the Media City

Steven Shaviro
No Speed Limit: Three Essays on Accelerationism

Jussi Parikka
The Anthrobscene

Reinhold Martin
Mediators: Aesthetics, Politics, and the City

John Hartigan Jr.
Aesop's Anthropology: A Multispecies Approach

Burgers in Blackface
Anti-Black Restaurants Then and Now

Naa Oyo A. Kwate

University of Minnesota Press

MINNEAPOLIS

LONDON

Published by the University of Minnesota Press, 2019
111 Third Avenue South, Suite 290
Minneapolis, MN 55401–2520
http://www.upress.umn.edu

The University of Minnesota is an equal-opportunity educator and employer.

Contents

Introduction

"SLAVES WERE AUCTIONED OFF the week of February 21, during noon. The student body bid . . . with the highest bidder getting the person for their slave on the assigned day . . . This was the 2nd year the student council held this money raiser, which made over 1,000 dollars this year." So read the 1978 yearbook feature describing "Sambo Service Day" at St. John's High School, Delphos, Ohio. Photo captions identified images of grinning White students who had "won" one of their peers, and others who were consigned to servitude. One of the latter group had adorned his shirt with masking tape that read, "Ain't I Cute?" The story text noted that "wearing signs is one way masters let people know who their slave is."[1] Making a mockery of slavery was apparently a new annual event at the parochial school, one in which the word "Sambo" stood for African Americans.

On the opposite end of the country, in Modesto, California, another all-White student body engaged in the same ritual. Fall

1. *St. John's High School Yearbook—1978*, page 21. Delphos, Ohio, 1978. https://records.myheritagelibraryedition.com/research/record-10568–161248136/st-johns-high-school, U.S. Yearbooks, 1890–1979, MyHeritage.com.

at Modesto High School meant the "traditional Slave Day." In 1979, "each Rally Exec was assigned to a varsity football player, and served as his slave for the day."[2] Where the Modesto celebration of slavery differed from that in Ohio was in an external connection to Sambo. The teens at St. John's merely named their event "Sambo Service Day," but in Modesto, each "slave" took her "master" to breakfast at Sambo's Restaurant, a West Coast pancake chain. Had these students deliberately chosen Sambo's as the setting for breakfast because the name and the chain's branding was ideally matched to an enactment of enslaved Black persons? As will be shown in the pages that follow, Sambo's Restaurant, which initially launched in California in 1957, was but one of several establishments where racism was integral to the dining concept.

This book examines the ways in which American restaurants have traded on denigrating images of Black people in names, branding, and architecture. The United States has a long history of Black stereotypes being used to sell products, particularly packaged food; the "comic darky" and other images have been concentrated in American culinary ephemera in a way that is not the case in other cultures.[3] Brands such as Uncle Ben's rice and Mrs. Butterworth's syrup are familiar to American consumers, but a number of restaurants, unabashed in their mockery of Blackness, have remained largely unknown. From the early twentieth century to the present, restaurants have offered White consumers a dining experience seemingly made that much more appealing by the spice of racism.

2. *Modesto High School Yearbook—1979*, page 44. Modesto, Calif., 1979. U.S. School Yearbooks, 1900–1990 Ancestry.com

3. Woys Weaver, "The Dark Side of Culinary Ephemera: The Portrayal of African Americans," *Gastronomica: The Journal of Critical Food Studies* 6, no. 3 (2006): 76–81.

Four such restaurants are: Richard's Restaurant and Slave Market, in Berwyn, Illinois; Sambo's, originally based in Santa Barbara, California; The Coon Chicken Inn, originally based in Salt Lake City, Utah; and Mammy's Cupboard, in Natchez, Mississippi. Spanning the country's geography, social settings, and historical contexts, these restaurants are but a sampling of the numerous establishments that have operated with racist themes. For example, Johnny Weissmuller, star of the Tarzan movies, opened the Jungle Hut Restaurant in the late 1960s in Fort Lauderdale, Florida. Capitalizing on his silver screen fame, his concept featured "a native African influence in design, décor and food. The menu includes such items as 'Gorilla Burgers,' Tiger Taters,' 'Gator Dogs' and 'Mango Milk Shakes.'"[4] There was also a "Famous Pic-a-Ninny" barbecue restaurant that operated in the near-west suburbs of Chicago, but however successful it had been, the business was sold at a mortgage foreclosure auction in 1939.[5] Aunt Jemima's Kitchen, which formed a franchise and began building outlets in the summer of 1960, capitalized on the caricature of a jolly and good-tempered mammy, and took it to scale. Aunt Jemima had already been successfully employed to sell pancake flour by suggesting that buyers could obtain the status of the plantation South (including Black labor) in a simple packaged mix; it was a slave in a box.[6] In the restaurant, con-

---

4. "Franchise File," *Fast Food Magazine* (October 1969).

5. Classified advertisement, *Chicago Tribune*, October 21, 1939, 26. Accessed October 11, 2017. https://www.newspapers.com/image/194920865.

6. M. M. Manring, *Slave in a Box: The Strange Career of Aunt Jemima* (Charlottesville: University of Virginia Press, 1998); Donald Bogle, *Toms, Coons, Mulattoes, Mammies & Bucks: An Interpretive History of Blacks in American Films,*. 3rd ed. (New York: Continuum, 2000); "Aunt Jemima's Kitchen Pancake Franchise Group Formed," *Fast Food Magazine* (1960), 58.

sumers could enjoy the double benefit of commodified Black stereotypes without having to cook themselves. Thus, the four restaurants examined here are illustrative case studies to explore how independent restaurants and national chains have sold the consumption of Black domination.

Racial formation theory and critical race theory are useful frames for making sense of the meaning behind these restaurants. Michael Omi and Howard Winant argue that racial categories are created and lived through racial projects, which define human bodies, social structures, and their interaction.[7] Always the outgrowth of previous historical conflicts, racial projects are the instruction manual for how everyday experiences ought to be organized around race. They are clearly visible in public policies (e.g., the state should be "color-blind"; Black males are suspect and should be stopped and frisked by police), but they operate in everyday lives as well: "Society is suffused with racial projects, large and small."[8] Racial projects make "common sense" out of the specific ways in which a racialized society is structured. Indeed, a racist society is itself common sense in the United States. According to critical race theory (CRT), racism is ordinary, not aberrational; it is the way society does business.[9]

Racist restaurants—their genesis and their persistence— constitute a racial project that normalizes racism by centering it in everyday consumption and making it a marketable good. By situating racism at the forefront of a space for children, families, and the pleasures of eating and sociability, racist restaurants seem

7. Michael Omi and Howard Winant, *Racial Formation in the United States: From the 1960s to the 1990s,* 2nd ed. (New York: Routledge, 1994).

8. Omi and Winant, 60.

9. Richard Delgado, and Jean Stefanic, *Critical Race Theory: An Introduction,* 3rd ed. (New York: New York University Press, 2017).

to dare the citizenry to take up critique. As CRT emphasizes, unconscious feelings motivated by national narratives about race strongly determine how individuals respond to racist cues. Racist marketing has particular resonance in the United States, where mass consumption has for decades been central to American identity and conceptions of a prosperous country.[10] Feeding into this larger racial project are smaller ones, which articulate several premises. The first is that racism does not necessarily pose a threat to society; in some contexts, it's all in good fun, a harmless joke. Second, racist expressions cannot be racism if Whites take simple pleasure from them. That is, racism is only construed as the expression of virulent hatred; merely enjoying the debasement of Black people falls short of the threshold for which we may levy claims of racism. And third, racism is purported to be no more than individual prejudice and bigoted attitudes, expressed and felt individually, on a case-by-case, ahistorical basis. Taken together, these "mini" racial projects are the building blocks that make possible a segment of the restaurant industry dedicated to antibBlackness. Because racist restaurants serve what CRT theorists would describe as the psychic and material needs of Whites, they have had remarkable longevity—an indication that they ought not be seen as bizarre one-offs but rather as a deeply rooted exemplar of common-sense American racism.

10. Lizabeth Cohen, *A Consumers' Republic: The Politics of Mass Consumption in Postwar America,* (New York: Knopf, 2003).

Coon Chicken Inn

THE COON CHICKEN INN was founded in 1925 in Salt Lake City, Utah, by Maxon and Adelaide Graham. Its namesake was the large grinning face of a Black man that formed the establishment's entrance. The Inn served a fairly pedestrian menu including oysters, ham and eggs, burgers, chili, sandwiches, and desserts, but its signature dish was Coon Fried Chicken, which came in several forms. When a new location opened in Seattle in 1930, it received prominent news coverage in the *Seattle Times*.

Realizing that the readership may not have understood what "Coon Chicken" meant, one article explained, "Anyone who has

Figure 1. The Coon Chicken Inn at 8500 Bothell Way, Seattle, Washington. The coon face is constructed differently in other pictures. For example, the facial expression is slightly different, and there is a bowtie at the neck. Source: Coon Chicken Inn Records and Graham Family Papers, Archives Center, National Museum of American History, Smithsonian Institution.

lived below the Mason-Dixon line knows that 'coon chicken' is the way the fowl is cooked by the real, old-fashioned southern mammy," a method that apparently produced crisp, grease-free chicken. Then is it coon chicken or mammy chicken? Is the coon married to the mammy? Otherwise, where are the plates of chicken coming from? It is interesting that the Inn's owners anticipated sufficient clientele for the restaurant when their patrons would generally not have lived "below the Mason-Dixon line," whence the brand's racial nostalgia is pulled. However, perhaps the Grahams recognized what Micki McElya has argued: that many Whites who lived in settings far removed from the American South "read hungrily and with pleasure" mythical tales of plantations replete with "black workers who 'knew their place' and the hospitality of rural plenty."[1]

The coon's derogatory portrayal of Black men—shuffling, shiftless, and stupid—is further dehumanizing because the name is taken from "raccoon."[2] By conflating two gendered stereotypes of Black people—mammy and coon—the restaurant foregrounds the perceived interchangeability of Black servitude and perceptions of natural Black affinity for chicken. Psyche Williams-Forson shows that after the Civil War, pictures became a primary means to remind Black people of their place in society. Postcards, posters, and other illustrations made Black people the butt of jokes, and one of these was the pervasive notion of their being chicken-lovers and especially stealers. Attempts at forging Black identities during Reconstruction were met with a psychic war

1. Micki McElya, *Clinging to Mammy: The Faithful Slave in Twentieth Century America* (Cambridge, Mass.: Harvard University Press, 2007), 11.

2. David Pilgrim, *Understanding Jim Crow: Using Racist Memorabilia to Teach Tolerance and Promote Social Justice* (Oakland, Calif.: PM Press, 2015).

waged in a variety of visual ephemera that circulated widely. These commodities of racism allowed the owner not only to own the image but also to "mentally covet" a depiction of Black people in which she or he had some investment.[3] Memorabilia from the late 1880s to the 1930s have been characterized as "symbolic slavery," created in a time when sharecropping, lynching, race riots, and other assaults on Black communities and Black lives were at an unprecedented level.[4] It was precisely in this context that the Coon Chicken Inn was born.

Everything about the Inn showcased the Black coon, the most prominent being the building itself. As *The Seattle Times* reported: "The building has been constructed to represent a southern log cabin. A huge replica of the head of a colored man, the official trade mark of the company, smiles from the front of the building displaying a row of gleaming white teeth." It is striking that the Grahams thought to require patrons to be (symbolically) consumed by a Black man. Perhaps the smiling face tempered the danger inherent in being swallowed whole. The logo reassures that this is just another buffoonish coon; patrons are to smile and laugh along. Americans were certainly accustomed to laughing at cartoonish Black men in various media, including on the big screen. Films such as *Rastus and Chicken, Pickaninnies and Watermelon,* and *Chicken Thief* were released between 1910 and 1911 and provided a shared understanding of Black men for Whites from various backgrounds.[5]

Apart from the building, there were napkins, dishware, and various promotional items that sported the grinning coon.

3. P. A. Williams-Forson, *Building Houses out of Chicken Legs: Black Women, Food, and Power* (Chapel Hill: University of North Carolina Press, 2006).

4. Williams-Forson, *Building Houses out of Chicken Legs.*

5. Bogle, *Toms, Coons, Mulattoes, Mammies, & Bucks.*

Figure 2. This promotional postcard displayed the locations for Seattle, Portland, and Salt Lake City, as well as the original building, which became a bakery and poultry farm. Each location was depicted with accurate drawings of the building. Source: Coon Chicken Inn Records and Graham Family Papers, Archives Center, National Museum of American History, Smithsonian Institution.

Figure 2 is a fold-out postcard that advertised the chain's different locations, each illustrated with a drawing of the gaping coon at the front door. The restaurant sold "Coon Head Ash Trays" to go along with the cigarettes available for purchase at the counter. And of course, the menu was replete with coon mentions. The "Coon Chicken Special," at $1.50 included french fries, salad, and hot buttered Parkerhouse rolls and preserves; for $.50 more, patrons could partake of the "Coon Chicken Dinner," which came with consommé, fruit, or chef's salad. For those with modest appetites, the "Baby Coon Special" comprised a half chicken. The menu itself was shaped in the outline of the coon's face and opened outward in two book pages. In some, the middle spine featured the same grinning coon, this time with a full body, dressed in an elegant and formal waiter's uniform and carrying a tray on which a chicken was the centerpiece.[6]

The restaurant had enjoyed several successful years in Salt Lake City before branching out to Seattle. "Coon Chicken Inn Opened in Seattle" blared a newspaper headline, with a large wide-angle photo titled, "UNUSUAL DINING RESORT SERVES PUBLIC." Coon Chicken Inn was positioned as a unique and in- novative venue, part of a coast-to-coast chain. The newspaper seemed to take literally the restaurant's slogan—"Nationally Famous Coast to Coast"—but the restaurants themselves did not have any locations east of the Mountain Time Zone. Although the story was accompanied by a photo of the restaurant façade, readers could get a better view of the smiling coon in the three- quarter page ad that invited potential diners, much like that shown in Figure 3. Between the articles, contractors herald- ing the restaurant opening (and thereby advertising their busi- ness), and the large display ad, the words and imagery of "Coon Chicken" absolutely dominated the newspaper's page.[7]

A plot on Seattle's Bothell Highway could not have been more appropriate. As one newspaper advertisement showed, the long stretch of road was home to some of the busiest summer resort restaurants, many of which relied on southern motifs: Henry the Watermelon King sold southern melons; there was a Dixie Inn; and a place called Mammy's Shack, "Said to be the origi- nators of the chicken-on-toast idea all cooked by a real south- ern mammy."[8] This trope of authenticity for chicken fried by a

6. Coon Chicken Inn Records and Graham Family Papers, 1913– 1973, Archives Center, National Museum of American History, Box 4, Folder 2. Undated. Restaurant menu.

7. Coon Chicken Inn Records and Graham Family Papers, Box 4, Folder 4. 1930. The *Seattle Sunday Times,* August 30, 1930, page 15.

8. Coon Chicken Inn Records and Graham Family Papers, Box 4, Folder 2. Undated. "Epicurean's Guide" (newspaper infographic).

Figure 3. A newspaper advertisement that appeared in the Oregon Daily Journal, September 11, 1933, announced the opening of the Portland location. The text began, "Well folks, here I am in Portland and all ready to serve you the finest chicken you have ever eaten. N.O. Eklund leased me the ground for my building and then built it, and what a place it is!" It is unclear whether the coon or the owner is speaking. Source: Coon Chicken Inn Records and Graham Family Papers, Archives Center, National Museum of American History, Smithsonian Institution.

southern mammy was deeply ingrained in American culture at this time, particularly in the South. By the late 1930s, foundations had been laid for new cooking technologies and domestic science, seen in cookbooks and schools, and all but the poorest kitchens followed suit. The South was shifting to be more in line with national norms in several domains, including national consumer culture, and White southerners felt this as a loss. As a result, southern cookbooks began to look to the past, seeking historical connections and idealized images of domesticity. The conception of Black people having intuitive and artistic skills in food preparation was front and center. White supremacy in the American South "interpreted black practices to be unchanging and immutable," and the emphasis on Black women's domestic labor served to "denigrate African American women and thereby validate the common white trope that connected blackness to service and common labor."[9]

Angela Jill Cooley argues that Black women's kitchen labor was essential in preserving White women's class and race privilege, and although the mammy image had long been used to sell foodstuffs, it became more prevalent in cookbooks and newspaper articles. Mammy was now the authority on homemaking and cooking skills, and that portrayal assisted the south in retaining regional distinctiveness as the rest of the country moved more toward a national consumer market. By 1935, Jim Crow had been firmly established across the South, precluding any fears about a contaminating threat to racial purity posed by Black servants. Instead, the notion that a Black woman's natural place in kitchen service came to the fore. Black women supposedly had an "inherent ability to cook" and "their service to whites is preordained

9. Angela Jill Cooley, *To Live and Dine in Dixie: The Evolution of Urban Food Culture in the Jim Crow South* (Athens: The University of Georgia Press, 2015), 75.

by God."[10] Indeed, it was not only Black women that were suited for kitchen work, the broader understanding was that African Americans as a whole were naturally servile.

In 1933, the Coon Chicken Inn was reviewed in *Western Restaurant*. Lauded for expansion plans while other restaurants were contracting in a difficult economic climate and reportedly voted most popular restaurant at the Roosevelt High School (it is unclear who voted and conducted the poll), the inn was flourishing. Customers often braved hours-long lines, the Seattle outlet was selling anywhere from one-half to two tons of chicken per day, and the overall chain pulled in half a million dollars the year prior, doing brisk business with Mormon organizations in Salt Lake City in particular. Soon it would be headed to Denver and the San Francisco metropolitan area.[11] In the meantime, the Coon Chicken Inn opened the "Club Cotton" in its basement, further capitalizing on selling Blackness to an audience in the American West. The nightclub was a "hit."[12]

Roy Hawkins, an African American man who migrated west during the Second World War and became a lead waiter at the Coon Chicken Inn, attributed the restaurant's success partly to its frying chicken whole, and partly to its logo, which was appealing to children and families. For Hawkins, while the coon imagery was hurtful, it was nothing compared to the racial terror he had endured in Texas. "From southern places and things, it wasn't nothing to see mockery. Black folks was always mocked … Now, I would be upset if somebody call me a Coon." Still, work-

10. Cooley, 83.
11. James R. Ferguson, "THE COON CHICKEN INN Expands during Depression," *Western Restaurant*, May 1933. Coon Chicken Inn Records and Graham Family Papers, Box 4, Folder 2.
12. Richmond Hurd, "Club Cotton–Another Hit for Coon Chicken Inn," *Western Restaurant*, April 1934. Coon Chicken Inn Records and Graham Family Papers, Box 4, Folder 2.

ing there meant more than having to abide racist symbols; that debasement was often brought into customer interactions. White diners referred to Black staff as "real live" coons and used other racial epithets in their presence.[13] But Hawkins felt he had the last laugh, as he would often take home between $100 and $200 in tips each night. In contrast, White bricklayers earned $5.00 per day. Hawkins also supervised several other Black wait staff, but these employees often quit, chafing under an openly racist environment. For some diners, Hawkins and other waiters were no more men than the caricature that grinned up at them from their china, napkins, and elsewhere around the room.[14] Indeed, the restaurant branding implied that its dining room was a "racism zone," an arena in which patrons could engage freely in racist behaviors, in which nothing would be off the table.

The restaurant closed in the 1950s, and little is available in archival sources to explain why. But the racism that was the centerpiece of the restaurant's operation persisted in cultural memory for decades afterward. In 1972, the *Trolley Times,* a small community periodical published in Salt Lake City, printed an article recounting the restaurant's history and showcasing a photograph of restaurant waitresses including LaVinnia Cook, head waitress for twenty-eight years. The article was written as a fictional first-person account by a Black grandfather. He spoke to his grandson of the olden days, and the text was therefore written in a stereotypical Black dialect. Grandpa began, "I was ridin' out de Highland Drive yestiddy en my mem'ry comes 'cross de Coon Chicken Inn. Seems like dat ol' coon head jist sort o' winked at me ag'in like it a'ways done. En I'll be dad blamed if'n I didn't just wink right on back. I reckon de past ain't all full o' meaness.

---

13. Williams-Forson, *Building Houses out of Chicken Legs.*
14. Williams-Forson, *Building Houses out of Chicken Legs.*

You got to laugh at some parts too." Thus, Grandpa reassured his true audience—White readers—that racism could be in good fun and ought not be taken so seriously. This was a recurring theme in the discourse surrounding restaurants like the Coon Chicken Inn. Grandpa continued by explaining that the Grahams were shrewd indeed to have developed this restaurant concept, and that the effective presentation made diners feel they had gone straight to the South for their meal. Grandpa was particularly praiseworthy of the coon icon: "See, he didn't build no ordinary do'way. At de end of his rest'rant, he 'structed a big, smilin' coon. Smilin' en winkin! 'Cross his white teef it said, 'COON ICKEN INN.' You couldn't see no CH on a 'count o' his front teef was cut out fo' de do'. So you stept ove' de bottom lip en right through his front teef en dere you was, a stan'in' on his tongue. Seemed sort a queer, stan'in' dere, knowin' you was 'bout to walk into de coon's belly, en things was all red en dark." Alas, the restaurant could not last forever. "In de 50's, dat's when de times started kickin' up a fuss 'bout de way we was gittin' treated unequal. Bimemby, de white folks in Washington, dey started knowin' too dat things wasn't completely fair. De Supremest Court en Mr. Eisenhower started writin' de Civil Rights Laws." In the view of what was coming down the pike (presumably equality for Black citizens, which was in no way realized during the Eisenhower administration), Graham saw "what was in de wind en dat coon head," and, having had enough of the business, decided to sell out.[15]

As late as 1970, Salt Lake County was 0.52% Black, a context in which the public ridicule of Black people in published media must have been unremarkable. At a minimum, the Inn's owners found this work innocuous, having seen fit to include it in

15. Lorraine Miller, "De Coon Chicken Inn," December 1972, *Trolley Times,* Coon Chicken Inn Records and Graham Family Papers, Box 6, Folder 4.

the company scrapbooks used to document their business. As Richard Delgado and Jean Stefanic argue,

> Our society has blithely consumed a shocking parade of Sambos, coons, sneaky Japanese, exotic Orientals, and indolent, napping Mexicans—images that society perceived at the time as amusing, cute, or worse yet, true. How can one talk back to messages, scripts, and stereotypes that are embedded in the minds of one's fellow citizens and, indeed, the national psyche? Trying to do so makes one come off as humorless or touchy.[16]

Indeed, time and again, White people with psychic and material investment in racist restaurants have portrayed the dehumanizing of Black people as something innocent, good-natured, and fun. Those who reject these images are seen as humorless at best, and as mendacious, militant threats to the social order at worst.

16. Delgado and Stefanic, *Critical Race Theory*, 82.

Mammy's Cupboard

OF THE FOUR RESTAURANTS discussed in this book, two are still in operation: Mammy's Cupboard and Sambo's. The former, as shown in Figures 4 and 5, is a restaurant building in Natchez, Mississippi, is an enormous Black woman into whose skirts patrons enter in order to have a meal. She is a larger-than-life roadside version of the genuine, old-fashioned southern mammy that the Coon Chicken Inn personified to those Seattle journalists. Like other images of Black women, she remains timeless and constant in a plain dress and head wrap."[1]

A Mississippi journalist imagined (and dispelled the notion) that "with her bosomy figure . . . the building looks as though she might have been imagined by a dirty-minded white 'massa.'" Whether the building realized the racial-sexual fantasies of the restaurant owner, we will never know, but it is clear that the idea of a buxom Black mammy is long lived in the American imaginary. Central to her longevity is the wish for White Americans to live in a world where Black folks, content to remain in faithful service, have long since shrugged off any anger about past (and present) injustices in which Whites are

1. Cooley, *To Live and Dine in Dixie*.

Figure 4. Mammy's Cupboard Restaurant, Natchez, Mississippi, before the restaurant was restored in 1980. Photograph by Carol M. Highsmith. Library of Congress, Prints & Photographs Division, reproduction number LC-DIG-highsm-13271.

Figure 5. Mammy's Cupboard, side view, Route 61, Natchez, Mississippi. Mississippi Natchez United States, 1979. Photograph by John Margolies. Retrieved from the Library of Congress, https://www.loc.gov/item/2017702209/.

complicit.[2] The architecture of Mammy's Cupboard took Aunt Jemima's "Slave in a Box" to the next level, enabling White patrons to consume Mammy's labor so completely that she does not merely prepare the food with her bare hands, her whole body is tasked with it. She is not only in the business of frying chicken, she *is* the business.

Launched in 1940, the restaurant was created by Henry Gaude. Some popular discourse locates the genesis of Mammy's Cupboard in Gaude's seeking to capitalize on the craze for *Gone with the Wind*. In this telling, the building was initially designed as a White Southern belle, and only later was transformed into a Black woman because "black was better than white in the road-food visual shorthand of 1940 Natchez, conveying ideas of nurturing and nourishment."[3] But this differs from other accounts, including journalistic reports based on interviews with those closest to the restaurant's operation. There, the focus on making a Black mammy is explicit and linked to the legacy of slavery. In any case, the Southern belle explanation ignores the context in which Black women are asked to nurture those who subordinate them, and accepts uncritically why a Black woman would be visual shorthand for food preparation. R.T. Davis, the businessman behind the Aunt Jemima brand, anticipated that a Black woman would be useful as the public face of his new pancake mix; here again with Mammy's Cupboard, a Black woman is used to stand in for prepared foods. Many Southern restaurants went to great lengths to portray an atmosphere redolent of Black servitude as a way to convey authenticity.[4]

2. McElya, *Clinging to Mammy*.
3. Nita Moser, 2016. "Field Review: Mammy's Cupboard, Natchez Mississippi," 2016, http://www.roadsideamerica.com/story/3344 (accessed December 6, 2017).
4. William Woys Weaver, *Culinary Ephemera—An Illustrated*

The more frequently recounted history is that Gaude and his wife meant for the restaurant to serve as a welcome station for visitors to the Natchez pilgrimages. These seasonal events provide public tours of privately-owned antebellum homes. In other words, homes that trace their grandeur to the wealth of the slave trade. Gaude's wife, a hostess for the pilgrimages, thought a restaurant and gas station shaped like a Black woman would be in keeping with event, and would therefore attract attention and business.[5] Because the Natchez pilgrimages celebrated antebellum architecture, culture, and history, this roadside Mammy was an explicit tribute to the institution of slavery. David Sullivan, the country's leading expert on the Black Consumer Market, produced his pioneering market research too late to inform the Gaudes. In 1943, he wrote an essay directing corporations to avoid depicting "colored women as buxom, broad-faced, grinning Mammies and Aunt Jemimas."[6]

As late as 1980, local media were sympathetic to this the idea of Mammy as cultural icon of Southern hospitality: "After tours of the antebellum homes where ladies and gentlemen once sipped mint julep and dined on barbecue, there's one more site here keenly reminiscent of the Old South. A traveler hasn't fully experienced Mississippi unless he has been by Mammy's Cupboard. . . . Like the stereotyped mammies of pre-Civil War days, she nurses chil-uns now aged into good ol' boys and gals.

History, (Berkeley: University of California Press, 2010).

5. "Tastes of Mammy's Cupboard Linger," *The Clarion-Ledger Jackson Daily News,* September 28, 1980, F; Margaret Nagle, "Adams County's Grand Lady Still Cooking after 42 Years," *The Clarion-Ledger,* October 14, 1982, https://www.newspapers.com/image/183583383 (accessed November 4, 2017).

6. Robert E. Weems *Desegregating the Dollar: African American Consumerism in the Twentieth Century* (New York: New York University Press, 1998).

They gather in her skirts every day for their fried chicken, home-made French fries and the happy hour."[7] This reporter could not have made a more pointed statement of the symbolic value of a Black mammy for White nurturance and sustenance.

At that time, Mammy's was owned by Edwin A. and Mildred Vedrenne. Edwin, Gaude's nephew, purchased the restaurant with his wife Mildred after it had closed in 1943, remaining shut-tered during World War II due to gas rationing. The Vedrennes operated the restaurant for nearly forty years, seeing it through at least one major challenge to its existence, when it was threatened by highway expansion in 1980. The Vedrennes sold restaurant souvenirs that allowed patrons to take mementos of slavery nos-talgia into their homes. Reported the *Clarion-Ledger* in Jackson, Mississippi, "Made from Mrs. Buttersworth bottles, 'Mammy' lamps and dolls with baskets of cotton atop their heads are sold to people from as far away as Switzerland, England, and Canada." The accompanying photo is captioned, "SOUVENIRS— Mrs. Butterworth syrup bottles have been painted and baskets of cotton attached to their heads to be sold to customers."[8] Mrs. Butterworth, already brown, has been recolored black, and as noted, has been adorned with material evidence of her enslaved labor. The dolls bring into jarring relief the extent to which the restaurant business sought to purposefully represent its business as the subjugation of Black bodies.

In 1982, Mildred offered to sell the establishment to a regu-lar customer, Judy Reeder. Mammy's was still a tourist draw in Natchez and was on the National Register of Historic Places. Reeder was interested in the purchase as much for its business potential as for her emotional connection to the restaurant. She

7. "Tastes of Mammy's Cupboard Linger," F.
8. "Tastes of Mammy's Cupboard Linger," F.

quipped, "I called it *Black Mammy's* as a child . . . I've always been fond of this place . . . Tourists still come in here who have been several times. They say they just had to stop by and see Aunt Jemima" (emphasis mine). As with the conflation of coon and Mammy, this slippage between Mammy's Cupboard and Aunt Jemima as brands reveals the underlying messaging of interchangeable Black servitude. And Reeder's adding "Black" to the name as a child makes clear the deeply embedded racial meaning of mammy. Mammy-as-building wielded significant power in solidifying racial understandings. With Mammy as part of the physical landscape, the built environment is a racial project, teaching residents (particularly children) what Blackness means. Reeder bought the restaurant and was mentored by Mildred Vedrenne in running the business until Vedrenne died a few months later. Reeder cited their relationship as motivation to "keep many of the traditions of Mammy's Cupboard, right down to the glass case with shelves of dolls dressed in the Southern tradition."[9] The Southern tradition for Reeder and her customers meant to make Black womanhood synonymous with slavery.

Historic preservationists have seen Mammy's Cupboard as an exemplar of a noteworthy but soon to be extinct vernacular architecture. Keith Sculle, who coauthored *Fast Food: Roadside Restaurants in the Automobile Age,* was in 1988 the coordinator of educational programs for the Illinois Historic Preservation Society. Asked to comment for a newspaper article that described Mammy's Cupboard as "a multi-storied brick-and-stucco replica of a black kitchen slave," Sculle argued that people often looked down on or disregarded such buildings because of their local character and lack of distinctive architectural heritage. In his

9. "Tastes of Mammy's Cupboard Linger," F; Nagle, "Adams County's Grand Lady Still Cooking after 42 Years."

words, Mammy was "the kind of thing that captures everyone's attention even though the locals oftentimes look down their noses at it . . . Why save these? They're just eyesores . . . let's bulldoze 'em down and put up a shopping center."[10] Sculle's reasoning elides key reasons why locals may have had negative feelings about Mammy's, none of which had anything to do with snobbery. While Mammy could be described as an eyesore, she is more offensive to hearts and minds. Some locals are Black, and do not wish to see replicas of "kitchen slaves" as roadside restaurant façades. We may look to Nicholas Powers's description of his reaction to Kara Walker's *A Subtlety* for the feelings that a giant Mammy may evoke. Walker's sculpture, a 2014 public art installation of a forty-foot Black female sphinx made out of sugar in the soon-to-be-demolished Domino Sugar factory in Brooklyn, New York, elicited the following from Powers: "Of course we both marveled at the immensity of the Mammy sphinx. Just the sheer size of it pushed us back on our heels. The physical weight of all that sugar, a symbol of the pain and profit wrung from our ancestors, our black bodies, fell on us hard."[11] So too would Mammy's Cupboard's fall hard on passersby. The physical scale of the edifice, the representation of enslavement and the pain of Black women, and the use of racial caricature for capitalist gain would weigh heavily on Black minds.

In the 1990s, Doris Kemp purchased the restaurant, which was falling into disrepair. She "introduced a menu of Mammy-cooked home-style meals: no burgers or fried food." In Kemp's view, the restaurant was popular because patrons associated it with their

10. Dewey Webb, "Tracking the Elusive 'Look at Me!' Buildings," *The Courier Journal,* July 25, 1988, https://www.newspapers.com/image/110510957 (accessed November 22, 2017).

11. Nicholas Powers, "Why I Yelled at the Kara Walker Exhibit," *Indypendent,* June 30, 2014.

childhoods, though this would only apply to White childhoods. Kemp discounted the idea that Mammy was racially divisive as a marketing tool: "She suffered a bit during the 1960s, with civil rights unrest, but most people don't think of her as racial." What Kemp means is "racist"—"racial" is a linguistic palliative used to take the sting out of the violence inherent in the word "racism." Kemp is not suggesting that Mammy has no race; that privilege of racelessness has only ever been accorded to people classified as White, a universal standard for humanity. Race is very much fundamental to who Mammy is, whether as a thirty-foot-tall building or in the everyday stereotypes that are so "common sense" that they cease to be perceived.

Kemp came to the restaurant after having bought a retirement home (a former plantation called Kingston Place) in Natchez with her husband and after having lived in Louisiana and thereafter, Warri, Nigeria. According to the journalist reporting on Kemp's story, her life in Africa played a role in preparing her for the restaurant endeavor. It is unclear whether the reporter was referring to Kemp regularly hosting dinners for dozens of people in Nigeria or whether Kemp's residency in West Africa was ideal for owning a restaurant in which the enslavement of Africans was a central motif.[12] But the restaurant changed hands yet again, and as of 2014, it was owned by Lorna Martin. She, too, was an apologist for the representation of the Black mammy, calling it a revered figure, one that continued to motivate customers to buy paraphernalia. Moreover, "some diehard visitors are 'disappointed that she's not still black.'"[13] The image of a mammy with a resolutely Black face was deeply ingrained in the American social fabric. In *Gone with the Wind*, the character Mammy is

12. "Mammy's Menu: Lunch, Memories," *Clarion Ledger*, February 21, 1996.
13. Moser, "Field Review."

"shining black, pure African, devoted to her last drop of blood to the O'Haras."[14] Musical recordings such as the advertisement for a new fox trot tune (Figure 6) also made specific reference to the severity of blackness in Mammy's skin tone.[15]

Whereas the face of Mammy's Cupboard became progressively lighter over the years, changing with each subsequent repainting (and reportedly starting after the near-miss with the highway),[16] the current restaurant owners made a decision to portray on the website the Black Mammy that patrons longed for. She is dark-skinned, with white hair, and holding out a tray. Strangely, the restaurant's website credits Kemp with opening the business in 1994, rather than simply taking over ownership of an establishment that had been doing business for nearly fifty years. Perhaps this is a way to distance the restaurant from a sordid Jim Crow history. Today, Martin and her daughter Tori Johnson are the current owners. The restaurant's website proclaims,

WELCOME TO MAMMY'S CUPBOARD! Mammy's Cupboard was built in 1940 and continues to stand as a much loved landmark on Hwy 61, South of Natchez, Mississippi. She is visited annually by local patrons as well as visitors from all over the world. Our home cooked food, desserts, and our specialty "Blueberry Lemonade," are enjoyed by many. Our motto is "Tourists treated same as home folk" and we strive to deliver down home service.[17]

As noted above, the website images made no compunction about presenting Mammy as dark-skinned, perhaps catering to a small-

14. Margaret Mitchell, *Gone with the Wind,* (1936; New York: Scribner, 2011), 43.

15. Advertisement, "Coal Black Mammy." *Evening Public Ledger,* October 27, 1922.

16. Moser, "Field Review."

17. "Welcome to Mammy's Cupboard." 2017, https://www.mammy-scupboard.com/home.html.

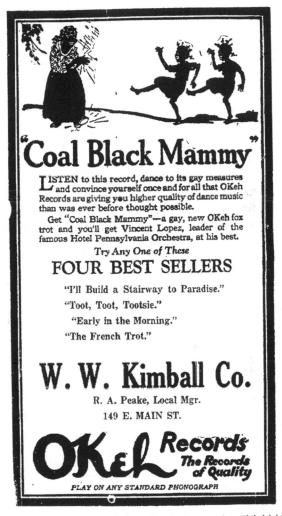

Figure 6. An advertisement from the Evening Public Ledger, Philadelphia, Pennsylvania, October 27, 1922. Source: https://chroniclingamerica.loc.gov/

er network of current customers, fans, and others who are sympathetic to an explicitly dark mammy. However, in more public settings—for example, on the consumer review website Yelp, the restaurant employs a more subdued image. There, the profile photo shows the more recent incarnation of Mammy, where her skin is light and she could be perceived as White.

Yelp reviewers were decidedly for or against, with few neutral views. Those against made frequent mention of racist iconography. Most of the positive reviews expressed sentiments about the "old-fashioned" atmosphere, and about enjoying the nods to an earlier era in American history and dining culture. This was an era in which the country's racial order was systematically writ into public spaces, and reviewers enjoyed looking back to that time via the depictions of Black servitude as "memorabilia" and cultural artifact. For example, "L.E.E." from Leicester, North Carolina found the establishment cute, "with bits of memorabilia on the walls," and recommended Mammy's Cupboard "to anyone looking for some good old fashioned food." Marie Y. from Dime Box, Texas, supported her written review with photos of Mammy, one of which was captioned, "Beautiful Mammy on this beautiful day!" Cathy C. from Wapakoneta, Ohio, noted, "What a throw back to the 60's. Remember these unique type of places when I was a kid." Both Kimberly L. from Webster, and Allan R., from Newport Beach, California, made reference to the restaurant's "kitsch." Allan stated, "If you are a lover of the kitschy roadside Americana (and I am) that is all too fast dying out, Mammy's Cupboard is a must visit. If nothing else, I always try to support these types of places, as once they are gone they seldom return." Roy M. of Pasadena, California, contended that "Eating here is like stepping back in time, to another era. How often do you have the opportunity to eat in the skirt of a 28-foot-high statue of Mammy?! Don't get me started." Others were more hesitantly pleased, unsure whether it was appropriate to appreciate the restaurant's themes but enjoying it nonetheless: David R from Winnetka, Illinois, said, "Came to see the unusual building (shaped like a "Mammy," not sure if that's even ok . . .), but loved the food!" Newspaper critics felt similarly: "We felt a little odd eating in a restaurant so insensitively shaped, but several people in Natchez had recommended Mammy's."[18]

Only one Yelp reviewer took exception at the restaurant's theme and imagery. Kim B., from Ypsilanti, Michigan, wrote in disgust, "I cannot believe a restaurant like this exist in 2017! You people are ignorant, racist bigots! Customers and owners. Then you have the nerve to have a gift shop filled with more racist relics! Unbelievable! You should be shut down ASAP!" Reviews available on Google were much more critical. Said Taneshia Powell-O'Neal, "Is no one alarmed by the fact that this restaurant is in the shape of a black mammy and they sell black mammy magnets in the gift shop? Do you know what a mammy is?" Quetzalcoatl wrote, "This is the most racist putrid restaurant I've ever seen. A mammy was a slave who was forced to breast-feed white children at the expense of her own children." Sierra Smith commented, "Racist, why would you build a restaurant basically making fun of black people. Go Away." Finally, Kirby McKay stated, "This is one of the most racist things I've seen. An old African slave as the building and also selling slave mammy dolls." Perhaps these reviewers failed to appreciate the reverence that White diners held for Mammy. It's something "that its later critics may have missed."[19]

18. ."In Search of American Pie," *The Journal News,* August 5, 1988, https://www.newspapers.com/image/164394479 (accessed November 4, 2017).

19. Moser, "Field Review."

Richard's Restaurant and Slave Market

THOUGH NOT AS WIDELY KNOWN or acclaimed as Mammy's Cupboard, Richard's Restaurant and Slave Market at 3011 South Harlem Avenue in the inner-ring Chicago suburb of Berwyn, appeared to have a fairly large and dedicated following. Berwyn, to the west of Chicago, is adjacent to Cicero, a town infamous for the virulent racism put on display to receive Martin Luther King Jr. in 1966. One Berwyn resident, Linda Dudek, was a second-grade student there in the late 1960s, and she recalled the sentiments of one of her seven-year-old classmates following Dr. King's assassination: "that nigger had it coming."[1]

Berwyn was a sundown town, a municipality in which local customs and/or laws forbade Black persons (and in some instances, members of other racial or ethnic groups) from remaining in town after dark, under threat of arrest, violent expulsion, or worse.[2] When Richard's opened in 1952, not a single Black person resided in any of the town's census tracts.[3] Forty years

---

1. James W. Loewen, *Sundown Towns: A Hidden Dimension of Segregation in America* (New York: New Press, 2005), 311.

2. Loewen, *Sundown Towns*.

3. Social Explorer. "Census Tract Data." https://www.socialexplorer.com/c4e465154d/view.

later, one family, the Campbells, bought a house in Berwyn. The family, parents and children alike, were greeted with arson and other threats of violence. City officials paid little mind, and the family soon moved out. According to the 1990 census, as the twentieth century drew to a close, only fifty-four Black people called Berwyn home.[4]

It was in this milieu of state-sponsored and sanctioned racism that Joseph and Helen Wilkos opened Richard's Restaurant and Slave Market. The restaurant was a family affair, with several adult children and spouses working in various capacities. Of the Wilkos's four children, Robert, Delores, and twins Josephine and Patricia, all except Delores worked at the restaurant. As well, both Josephine's and Patricia's husbands were employed at Richard's. An eBay listing for a menu shows that customers were offered a variety of dishes. One of the daily specials for Wednesday luncheon was "Polish Sausage, Red Cabbage," while regular menu items included "Lobster Tail with Drawn Butter" ($3.25) and "Roast Beef" ($3.00). The menu selections and prices suggest that the Wilkos family was courting a well-to-do clientele, and promotional postcards to women planning weddings made the same point. One featured interior photographs and the following text: "CONGRATULATIONS BRIDE TO BE. Picture your reception in one of our four beautiful rooms, alive with color that will flatter your beauty. Reflect your good taste for food. Our reputation for pleasing the most discriminating of people is your insurance." An ironic choice of word—"discriminating"—to describe those who would enjoy the notion of dining at a slave market.

It is unclear whether the restaurant was born as Richard's Restaurant and Slave Market or if the reference to slavery was

4. Loewen, *Sundown Towns.*

added at a later date; a 1959 *Yellow Pages* ad lists the establishment only as Richard's Restaurant and Cocktail Lounge, and postcards (see Figures 7 and 8) used the same appellation. Duncan Hines's 1959 *Adventures in Good Eating,* a guidebook to restaurants around the country, merely listed the establishment as "Richard's." By the early 1960s, however, "Slave Market" had replaced "Cocktail Lounge" in advertisements. The name, brazen in its celebration of abject Black personhood, is singular even within a genre of restaurants that used blatant racism to market their products. It was not an unmarked "speakeasy" type of establishment, where only a few were privy to the name and its operation. The name was generally known and displayed widely. As noted above, the establishment advertised in the *Yellow Pages,* was reviewed in the press, ran classified ads, and was the venue for the meetings of area organizations. For example, the Chicago chapter of the Alfa Romeo Owners Club called a meeting and shortened the restaurant name to a parsimonious "Richard's Slave Market, 3011 South Harlem Avenue." The meeting included a cocktail hour, dinner, election event, and road racing films as entertainment.[5]

In some instances, however, news coverage omitted the "Slave Market" portion of the brand. For example, the *Chicago Tribune* reported in 1964 that "Richard's Restaurant" had been bombed with dynamite, leaving the community in chaos. James Smith, an employee who was injured and the only one to appear in the article's photos, must have been one of the few Black individuals allowed in Berwyn during daylight hours. A porter, Smith was working in the kitchen when an explosion shook the roof and

---

5. Classified advertisements. *Chicago Tribune,* November 14, 1965, https://www.newspapers.com/image/201664572, (accessed November 4, 2017).

Figure 7. Postcard view of Richards Restaurant & Lounge in Berwyn, showing an exterior and interior view." Source: James R. Powell Route 66 Collection/ Postcards from Rt. 66, Newberry Library, Chicago.

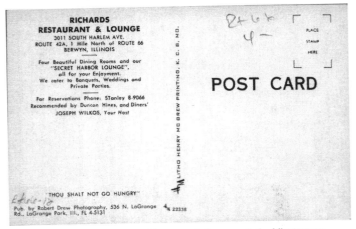

Figure 8. The mailing side of the postcard above reveals the following text: "Four Beautiful Dining Rooms and our 'SECRET HARBOR LOUNGE,' all for your Enjoyment. We cater to Banquets, weddings and Private Parties." After identifying Joseph Wilkos as the owner ("host"), the tagline reads, "THOU SHALT NOT GO HUNGRY." Source: James R. Powell Route 66 Collection/ Postcards from Rt. 66, Newberry Library, Chicago.

rained debris upon him and a coworker.[6] The Wilkos's other establishments had also been bombed on other occasions, including the Lulu-Belle, hit by a gasoline bomb, and Richard's Lilac Lodge, in the community of Hillside, destroyed to the tune of $600,000. Officials suspected that the bombing campaign stemmed from Wilkos and other restaurant owners' 1958 testimony before Senate committee hearings on rackets. As a result, Berwyn neighbors had "been sort of expecting this." For his part, Wilkos's twenty-six year-old son and restaurant manager Robert announced he was hiring private guards and would order them "to shoot first and ask questions afterward."

6. George Bliss, "3D Bomb for Cafe Owner," *Chicago Tribune*, September 2, 1964.

The Lilac Lounge was rebuilt in 1967 and co-owned by Robert and Sandra Wilkos. The restaurant décor ("authentic African") featured wall-mounted animal heads, "all kinds of jungle trophies," a gun collection, and contained an "exotic Safari Room" where adventurous diners could enjoy an informal setting "from the Dark Continent." The menu, despite purportedly comprising "African entrees," featured meals with geographic referents far removed from any African country, including "Alaska King Crab," and "Poulet à la Kiev." Other entrees simply tacked on African-sounding labels: "Roast Duck Zambizi," "Shrimp Zanzibar," and "African Fried Chicken." Drinks were named more pointedly for standard tropes about Africa: "Elephant Walk," "Monkey's Delight," and "the Headshrinker."[7]

Other than the bombings, little about Richard's Restaurant and Slave Market appears in public discourse, save a few restaurant reviews, and the establishment was rather local in its reach. Unlike Mammy's, or as will be seen, Sambo's, archival sources do not reveal racial controversy over the name, nor are simple first-person narratives of patronage available. An eBay posting for an unsent postcard (sender's name illegible) told that, "We were here for dinner May 9 with Charline. Woody has been gone 3 yrs on that date. May 15, 1963."

Restaurant reviews (also labeled "advertisement," suggesting that the evaluations were commissioned and/or paid for by the Wilkos family) played up the sumptuousness of the settings at Richard's. In October 1964, Bud Marker wrote about its four

7. Roy Dehn, "A Reputation for Excellence: Richard's Lilac Lodge," *Chicago Tribune,* May 16, 1974, https://www.newspapers.com/ image/201435104 (accessed June 16, 2018); Sally McCormick, "It's an Adventure Dining in the Safari Room! Richard's Lilac Lodge," *Chicago Tribune,* September 30, 1971, https://www.newspapers.com/im-age/196848447 (accessed June 16, 2018).

rooms. The main dining room, geared towards family clientele, served a variety of entrees ranging from beef stroganoff and prime rib, to Cantonese beef and Chinese Egg rolls. The Royale Room, a "stately" banquet hall, was adorned with "aristocratic" fittings, while the Treasure Chest offered children's dining. Finally, there was the Slave Market, the restaurant's cocktail lounge. Here, "the cocktail waitress dressed in a slave girl costume, makes sure that service is quick and the drinks mixed to perfection."[8] While classified ads for waitstaff did indicate that costumes were prerequisite, no evidence is available to show what they looked like.[9] Marker also described the lounge as "exotic"—a frequent code for the otherness of Africa—and enjoined readers not to miss the twelve-by-seven-foot mural and slave-girl mannequin.

The restaurant remained popular into the late 1970s, its name a moving target. Whereas in earlier years, the restaurant proudly displayed the full name in *Yellow Pages* advertising, the 1971 *Chicago Yellow Pages* now excised "Slave Market," listing the business as Richard's Restaurant and Ballroom.[10] However, in other contexts, the restaurant retained the racist nostalgia that undergirded the business from its inception, and the public continued to enjoy it, calling the name "intriguing."[11] For example, to a more circumscribed audience, such as the *Oak Park Leaves* newspaper, the establishment continued to purvey itself with the full name, if slightly modified: Richard's Restaurant & Slave

8. Bud Marker, "Display Ad 118-Enjoy the Many Moods of Dining at RICHARD'S 30th and Harlem," *Chicago Tribune*, October 22, 1964.

9. Classified ads. *Chicago Tribune*, August 16, 1964, https://www.newspapers.com/image/201582741 (accessed July 12, 2017).

10. *Chicago's Yellow Pages* (Chicago: The Reuben H. Donnelly Telephone Directory Co., 1971).

11. "Richard's Restaurant and Lounge, 3011 S. Harlem, Berwyn, Ill.," *Chicago Tribune*, July 22, 1976, W7.

Market Lounge. The addition of "Lounge" clarifies that in fact no auction block is actually on offer.

After twenty-five years in business, Richard's was described as a landmark destination in Chicago's western suburbs, a venue of choice for a family's most intimate and festive occasions, and also a favorite dining location for political figures and celebrities.[12] Several presumably local performers made regular appearances in the Slave Market Lounge, including Jim Stein, guitarist, Bill Solar, pianist, and Wally Valentine on the Cordavox (accordion). Richard's was still hiring new kitchen staff as late as 1979, but closed along with the other Wilkos restaurants in 1980.[13] Available resources do not report the reason for the closure, but a series of deaths in the family may have played a role. Helen and Joseph Wilkos lost their son and restaurant manager Robert in 1971. The thirty-two-year-old died in a plane crash when two training flights collided in mid-air. Two years later Joseph died at age sixty-six at his winter home in Florida—away from his wife Helen—in 1973. Finally, Patricia and her husband John Vallerugo's college-aged son John Jr. died in a car accident in 1976.[14] Despite the business having grown substantially, over time, into a prosperous enterprise, accounts of what the restaurant's closure meant to local residents are unavailable, consonant

12. "Richard's Restaurant and Lounge, 3011 S. Harlem, Berwyn, Ill.," *Chicago Tribune,* March 19, 1977, W12.

13. "Helen T. Wilkos Kramer," *Chicago Tribune,* April 8, 1992, Obituaries, https://www.newspapers.com/image/389702778 (accessed May 30, 2018).

14. "John A. Vallerugo Jr.," *Chicago Tribune,,*May 18, 1976, Obituaries, https://www.newspapers.com/image/383905949 (accessed May 30, 2018); "Joseph Wilkos," *Chicago Tribune,* April 26, 1973, Obituaries, https://www.newspapers.com/image/376840716 (accessed May 30, 2018); "Robert E. Wilkos " *Chicago Tribune,* May 8, 1971, Obituaries, https://www.newspapers.com/image/197527629(accessed May 30, 2018).

with the few details divulged about the restaurant while it was open. The secrets of the Slave Market Lounge remain hidden other than that it drew its name from "the many paintings that adorn the walls."[15] It is chilling to imagine what kinds of images those were.

15. Mick Tierney, "A Restaurant for Diners of All Tastes and Parties of All Sizes: Richard's Restaurant & Lounge, 3011 S. Harlem, Berwyn," *Chicago Tribune,* January 13, 1979.

Sambo's

VINCE CULLERS, principal of the nation's first Black advertising agency, so infused his Chicago-based practice with Black pride that Black households clipped out his advertisements from magazines and hung them on their walls. Cullers attributed his firm's success to creating "ads in a way blacks prefer to be portrayed— proud black people who are also warm and understandable."[1] He advertised his advertising in Operation Breadbasket's 1969 Black Expo program booklet with a text-only buy. Rendered in crisp black text on a plain white background, the copy comprised a vertical list of colloquialisms that use black pejoratively, such as "black friday," "black heart," and "blackmail," followed by the tagline "white lies." Last in the list was "little black sambo."[2] Cullers's childhood would have coincided with the era when the children's story *Little Black Sambo* enjoyed nationwide popularity, and his aversion to this debasing image resonated with many other Black Americans across the country.

1. "Black Ad Agency Leads Way to Sales for Negro Market," *Chicago Daily Defender*, November 11, 1969,
2. W. Alvin Pitcher, Papers, [Box 1, Folder 8], Special Collections Research Center, University of Chicago Library, Operation Breadbasket Black Expo Program, 1969.

Sambo's is the most infamous of the restaurants discussed in this book. Much of its thirty-year run saw controversy and public protest. Launched in 1957 by Sam Battistone and Newell Bohnett as a pancake house in Santa Barbara, the company distinguished itself to potential franchisees by offering ownership incentives that would later prove unsustainable and be characterized as a pyramid scheme. The company eventually declared bankruptcy and closed almost half the stores before being bought out by another company in 1986.[3] Though financial issues were the company's undoing, at least some public commentary has held that the chain's controversies were at fault—specifically, that the zealous left unfairly took down the chain by playing the race card. Though the chain disputed the etiology of the name (discussed in detail later), saying it was an amalgam of Sam (Battistone) and Bo (hnett), it clearly came from *Little Black Sambo*, a story first published in 1899.

Little Black Sambo in Popular Culture

Helen Bannerman, a Scot, wrote the story en route back to India, having just left her two oldest children enrolled in English schools. As she sailed to reunite with her husband, Major Bannerman, she penned the story for her children. It was during the trip that "Sambo popped into her mind. She jotted down the story as it came to her, sketching pictures of the little boy to illustrate his adventures." But for a friend who encouraged her to publish the story, she would have discarded it.[4] The Bannermans

3. John A. Jakle and Keith A Skulle. *Fast Food: Roadside Restaurants in the Automobile Age* (Baltimore: Johns Hopkins University Press, 1999).

4. "Little Black Sambo Still Liked," *The Courier-Journal,* November 24, 1946. https://www.newspapers.com/image/107122843 (accessed October 12, 2017).

had lived in India for ten years at that time, and prior to their marriage, Helen had traveled extensively throughout the British empire with her father. Little Black Sambo was set in India—as her own life was—and Bannerman drew on colonial tropes in writing it. The "Black" in "Black Sambo" was at once adjective, taxonomy, given name, and heritage. Bannerman wrote several other stories of the "Little Black" appellation, including Little Black Quibba, Little Black Quasha, Little Black Bobtail, and Little Black Mingo.[5]

In attaching "Black" to Sambo, the author created a racial redundancy that served only to highlight and subordinate the character for his nonwhiteness. There was no disputing the meaning of Sambo in the British empire. Bannerman's title drew on a vocabulary of racism that was prominent in visual references and everyday language. The print "Massa Out. 'Sambo Werry Dry'" made by Henry Pidding, a British printmaker, painter, and draughtsman born in 1797, depicted a Black male servant sitting at a table and pouring wine into a glass, with a satisfied, relaxed, and mischievous grin on his face, as he speaks to the dog seated at his feet.[6] Sambo, in his tortured English, was explaining to his canine companion that having accessed the master's cellar, he was able to quench his thirst with wine. The image reveals Sambo—Black men—to be slothful and prone to duplicitousness and debauchery given the first opportunity. Other artist renditions of Sambo existed in the form of George Cruikshank's book illustrations. In these, Frank Heartwell, a White man, was ac-

5. Joseph Lelyveld, "Now Little White Squibba Joins Sambo in Facing Jungle Perils," *New York Times*, August 4, 1966.

6. Henry Pidding, "Massa Out. 'Sambo Werry Dry.'" Paper mezzotint etching, 1828. London. The British Museum, #1935,0522.3.195

companied by his friend Sambo, who is pitch black in the prints, and rendered with poorly distinguished features.[7]

Little Black Sambo quickly crossed the Atlantic to the United States.[8] In so doing, the story was assimilated into the country's racial hierarchy. *The Tennessean* published a large spread of the story in 1907 titled "Children's Stories That Never Grow Old: Little Black Sambo" (Figure 9). Here Bannerman's tale is told in full. Sambo is born of parents who embody foolishness; lacking real names, they are robbed of individuality and humanity. They are named Black Mumbo and Black Jumbo—together they are Mumbo Jumbo, a hot mess of nonsense. Black Mumbo (Sambo's mother) sewed his outfit, and his father Black Jumbo bought him a green umbrella. The text reads, "And Black Jumbo went to the Bazaar and bought him a beautiful Green Umbrella and a lovely little Pair of Purple Shoes with Crimson Soles and Crimson Linings. And then wasn't Little Black Sambo grand?"

It is debatable whether the reader is meant to answer yes. The question reads as rhetorical, suggesting that in fact Sambo is far from grand, but rather a fun-size version of the stereotypically buffoonish and uppity Black male trying and failing to clothe himself in the sartorial flair that is the province of his White counterparts. Cartoons of Black people routinely showed them posturing in ridiculous outfits and critiqued them for risible attempts to elevate themselves beyond their contemptible natural stations.[9] Little Black Sambo evokes Jim Crow, the character Thomas Rice portrayed in his minstrel act; dressed in eccentric

7. George Cruikshank, "George Cruikshank's Omnibus" (Frank Heartwell). Paper etching, 1842. London: Charles Tilt. The British Museum, #1978,U.2569

8. "Choice Juvenile Books," *New York Tribune,* December 15, 1900, https://www.newspapers.com/image/88137045 (accessed October 11, 2017).

9. Pilgrim, *Understanding Jim Crow.*

Figure 9. "Children's Stories That Never Grow Old" appeared in *The Tennesse-an*'s Sunday paper, September 15, 1907. Source: http://www.newspapers.com

garb, layered in accessories, colors, and textures, his appearance "was most ridiculous." Rice's performance purportedly drew from his observation of "an old decrepit slave named Jim Crow," an enslaved man who worked for a stable owner surnamed Crow. This Black man sang a song to himself and danced, punctuated by a little jump, and "was so frightfully deformed as to appear inhuman." Such was his physical constitution that one of the marked aspects of his comportment was a limp: "a pitiful, yet ludicrous, hobble." Thus audiences delighted in the privilege of mocking Black debility; welcoming a portrayal of a disfigured creature that was less than human.[10]

In the *Tennessean* strip, Sambo's face is concordant with widely purveyed images of Black people at that time—a shock of hair, large hoop earrings, an enormous mouth, gleaming white eyes that bulged in their sockets. His body is reminiscent of an old man's rather than that of a young boy. When he receives his new ensemble, he is naked, save for a short skirt, every bit the primitive, savage African. So robed, he ventures out into the jungle, where he is challenged by a tiger who wants to eat him. As Sambo debates the tiger, his face is contorted into a grotesque mask, with a mouthful of teeth echoing the tiger's. His hands are splayed and he is bent at the waist in an odd pose. Sambo successfully trades a piece of his clothing for his freedom, but the reprieve is short lived, and Sambo has to repeat the exercise several times with additional tigers.

After bartering away all his clothes, Sambo is disconsolate, having lost his finery, reduced to a loincloth of a dark grassy material. But soon the group of tigers begin fighting each other

10. Esther Cleophes Quinn, "'Jumped Jim Crow,' Reminiscences of Rice, the Father of Negro Minstrelsy," *Washington Post,* August 25, 1895; Frederic R. Sanborn, "'Jump Jim Crow!' The Opening of an Era," *New York Times,* November 13, 1932.

Figure 10. Jim Crow. London, New York, and Philadelphia: Published by Hodgson, 111 Fleet Street and Turner and Fisher between 1835 and 1845? Photograph retrieved from the Library of Congress, https://www.loc.gov/item/2004669584/.

over Sambo's clothes, and as they race each other around a tree, they reduce themselves to a puddle of butter. Sambo regains his clothes, is now shown as tall and muscular, and his hair appears in a kinkier mass. In profile, his face is essentially an eye and enormous lips. He is a threatening brute, not a hapless Sambo. The end of the tale is illustrated by pancakes piled high on a plate, accompanied by a small tub of "Tiger GHI" (presumably, "ghee"). Nothing about the story or illustration suggests that it was taking place in India. Inexplicably, the *Tennessean* closed out the spread with a footer comprising images of two simian-looking individuals standing between the open mouths of two alligators. This surplus denigration of Blackness makes reference to the common representation of Black children as alligator bait.[11]

Several knockoff editions of Bannerman's story emerged in the United States. "All About Little Black Sambo" was published in New York by Cupples & Leon Company in 1917. In this version, Sambo is short in stature but does not look like a child. He is coal black, shiny, with a large, white mouth rendered in thick outlines as would be a clown's mouth. Because he wears a coat and knickers but no shirt,[12] he evokes a flasher. He's not at all cute, and rather sinister. In another rendition, *The Story of Little Black Sambo*, published in 1910 by Reilly & Britton, the cover announces, "The Only Authorized American Edition." Figure 11 shows this book cover along with another edition, on display at the National Museum of African American History and Culture. Within the text, illustrations are color versions of those in the *Tennessean*. As seen in the photograph, on the cover the image is less of a caricature, but the stereotypical features are still distinguishable. Sambo's hair is straight in texture, but

11. Pilgrim, *Understanding Jim Crow*.
12. Pilgrim, *Understanding Jim Crow*.

Figure 11. U.S. editions of *Little Black Sambo* published by E. P. Dutton (1852) and J. B. Lippincott & Co., (1836–1978). Collection of the Smithsonian National Museum of African American History and Culture, Gift of the Collection of James M. Caselli and Jonathan Mark Scharer. Photographed by the author at the National Museum of African American History and Culture, Washington, D.C., in 2017.

sports loose curls. But inside the book, the images revert to the dehumanizing, beastly renditions shown in the *Tennessean*. Black Mumbo is rotund as before, holding a frying pan and a spoon, with dark skin, a wide, gap-toothed mouth with huge red lips that stretch the entire width of her broad face, and close-set eyes and nose. She wears a yellow polka-dot scarf over her hair, which is shown to be frizzled. She is barefoot with large feet and wearing a white apron with red polka-dots that match her lips.[13] She is animalistic.

It is important to note that these Sambo imprints were absolutely consonant with the depictions of Blackness in children's literature. Stories and illustrations minced no words in telling young readers that people of African descent were subhuman, objects of scorn and contempt. Thomas Edison introduced *Ten Pickaninnies* in 1904, photographing anonymous Black children who were referred to as "snowballs, cherubs, coons, bad chillun, inky kids, smoky kids, black lambs, cute ebonies, and chubbie ebonies."[14] On February 29, 1912, a resident of Dushore, Pennsylvania wrote in to the "Dear Elizabeth" column at the *Wilkes-Barre Times Leader, The Evening News*. This advice and information column had apparently been receiving many requests related to poetry, and this reader had a question in the same vein: "I would like to get the verses, part of it reads something like this: 'Ten little nigger boys going to dine, one got shot and then there was but nine.'" Elizabeth was able to furnish the poem that this reader sought, a Mother Goose rhyme first published in the late 1800s and remaining true to the original over time, for "Children like realism in art; they like their ten

13. Pilgrim, *Understanding Jim Crow*.
14. Bogle, *Toms, Coons, Mulattoes, Mammies & Bucks*, 7.

little niggers very black, their froggies-that-a-wooing go very green . . ."[15]

The poem started almost exactly as the reader remembered, and then recounted a series of incidents that systematically reduced the group of Black boys from ten to none. For example, "Seven little nigger boys chopping up sticks, One chapped [sic] himself in half and then there were six"; "Four little nigger boys went out to sea, A big herring swallowed one and then there were three"; and "Two little nigger boys sitting in the sun, One got shriveled up and then there was one."[16] In addition to the coarse depiction of violent deaths of Black boys, the verse rendered Black children as things to be counted (as during slavery), rather than as people.[17] Chatto and Windus, the British house that published *Little Black Sambo,* also published *Ten Little Niggers.* In the mid-1960s an editor there claimed, "These stories belong to an entirely different age. They're classically innocent. Certainly there's nothing malicious about them."[18]

In addition to Bannerman's tale, the Sambo image was popular in other storytelling. Not long after the publication of the Mother Goose nursery rhyme, *The Topeka State Journal* was running a regular comic strip with a protagonist named Sambo. It depicted him as per standard: black, simian-featured caricature. In one

15. "Mother Goose Hit for Racial Slurs," *Courier-Post,* April 3, 1969, https://www.newspapers.com/image/181354608 (accessed October 12, 2017); *The Guardian,* October 22, 1889, https://www.newspapers.com/image/259033721 (accessed October 12, 2017).

16. *Wilkes-Barre Times Leader, The Evening News,* February 29, 1912, https://www.newspapers.com/image/133098664 (accessed October 12, 2017).

17. Melissa F. Weiner, "(E)racing Slavery: Racial Neoliberalism, Social Forgetting, and Scientific Colonialism in Dutch Primary School History Textbooks," *Du Bois Review* 11, no. 2 (2014): 329–51.

18. Lelyveld, "Now Little White Squibba Joins Sambo in Facing Jungle Perils."

comic, Sambo heads to Australia "All fo' de pleasure ob his jet Black society."[19] In a 1909 narrative, Sambo is lassoed and trussed up in a rope by his nemeses, two White boys. They delight in dragging him across rough terrain and a river, with the noose around his neck ("Poor Sambo!" commiserates his pet dog). The reader is given every indication that he will be lynched—said one of the boys, "We'll tie him to a tree and leave him out to dry!"—but in the end he is tied standing up against a tree while animals of the forest crowd around what they perceive to be their dinner. Sambo manages to escape.[20]

Returning to Bannerman's story, M. Genevieve Silvester published a comic strip in serialized form, with a set of four frames appearing daily, so that children could collect them all and fashion their own booklet.[21] Once again, Sambo is utterly black in color, with white lips, eyebrows, and, in most images, white circles for eyes that contain no pupils—the empty circles end in the blackness of his skin. Sambo also has white circles elsewhere on his body, which at first blush would appear to be holes in clothing, but because he wears none, these unnamed wounds give him a further otherness. At home, he and his parents are the same color as the iron skillet that Black Mumbo wields while making their pancakes. And for good measure, there is a jar of molasses on the table, another item with which the family is

19. "Sambo's Off for the Land of the Kangaroo," *Topeka State Journal,* April 22, 1911, http://chroniclingamerica.loc.gov/lccn/sn82016014/1911–04–22/ed-1/seq-20/ (accessed December 6, 2017).

20. "Sambo and His Funny Noises," *Topeka State Journal,* March 6, 1909, http://chroniclingamerica.loc.gov/lccn/sn82016014/1909–03–06/ed-1/seq-9/ (accessed December 6, 2017).

21. M. Genevieve Silvester, "Little Black Sambo," *Bradford Evening Star and the Bradford Daily Record,* March 12, 13, 14, 15, 16, 17, 1928, https://www.newspapers.com/image/75897011 (accessed October 11, 2017).

equally matched in tone. Sambo's crude, blunt rendering—black skin and garishly contrasting facial features—place him at a lesser level than the tigers with whom he tangles; they are drawn with a fine-arts precision that gives them personality and clarity.[22]

Little Black Sambo deeply resonated with American children, parents, schools, libraries, critics, and anyone who paid attention to children's literature. Community and school groups routinely staged productions. An Indiana puppet club put on two performances in 1936, one of which was *Little Black Sambo*, and the other was "A Colonial Tea Party." The juxtaposition of these two plays illustrates the latent connections between Sambo and a colonial vision of Blackness.[23] Children at the Jackson School in Wisconsin staged a performance of *Little Black Sambo*, in which rudimentary costumes comprised paper masks, decorated to depict the story's characters. Horizontal stripes on a white background with small ears on the top were tigers; the youth playing Sambo wore a bag painted black, with white eyes, nose, and oversize lips.[24] The book had remained popular forty years after its release, and new editions continued to be produced. For example, in 1942 Grosset and Dunlap released "the well-loved nursery classic of that jaunty jungle boy, Little Black Sambo . . . now presented with modernized illustrations. These gay, new pictures can capture many new admirers for this favorite of many years."[25]

22. Silvester, "Little Black Sambo."

23. "M'Kinley 6A to Stage 2 Plays," *The Times*, February 13, 1936. https://www.newspapers.com/image/306501468 (accessed October 11, 2017).

24. "Jackson Pupils Act Story of Little Black Sambo." *Green Bay Press-Gazette*, January 6, 1940, https://www.newspapers.com/image/187566916 (accessed October 11, 2017).

25. *The Cincinnati Enquirer*, September 5, 1942, https://www.newspapers.com/image/100453945 (accessed October 11, 2017).

In sum, Sambo was a pervasive and well-understood denigration of blackness. The name, and the various characters that bore it were unequivocally Black and unequivocally negative. In fact, "Sambo" as a term connected to Black subordination was so well understood that White Americans frequently used it to name black animals. For example, in Salt Lake City, a monkey who nearly escaped captivity in a drive-in theater zoo bore the name, and in Mira Loma California, Mr. and Mrs. Charles Waite gave a foster home to a black sheep named Sambo.[26]

The Birth of a Nation's Restaurant Chain

It was in this context that the Sambo's chain launched in 1957 in California. Almost at the same time (1958), Ronald and Matilda Krieger's restaurant, named Lil' Black Sambo, opened in Oceanlake, a community in coastal Lincoln City, Oregon. It advertised seventeen varieties of pancakes and ten-cent coffee in 1959.[27] These advertisements for an apparently independent restaurant did not include any depictions of Sambo himself. However, the restaurant remains in business today as Lil Sambos, and the website (lilsambos.com) proudly acknowledges Bannerman's tale as the source, and defines the original name as Lil Black Sambos. The name change reflected changing times. According to the *Statesman Journal*, "The Li'l Black Sambo

---

26. "Big Monkey Makes a Try for Booze," *Petaluma Shopper*, November 23, 1960, https://www.newspapers.com/image/255409790 (accessed October 11, 2017); "Photo," *Los Angeles Times*, February 23, 1967, https://www.newspapers.com/image/165930746 (accessed October 11, 2017).

27. "Business Name Filed," *Corvallis Gazette-Times*, July 10, 1958, https://www.newspapers.com/image/146810494 (accessed October 12, 2017); classified advertisement," *Eugene Guard*, July 24, 1959, https://www.newspapers.com/image/146810494 (accessed October 12, 2017).

restaurant at the Oregon Coast has gone through a transformation wherein it became Li'l Sambo and its symbolic character has turned from black to white."[28] But newspapers continued to use the names interchangeably, inserting "Black" on different occasions. For example, the Lincoln City restaurant was to host a breakfast for the National Business Women's Week, and the location was given as "Lil' Black Sambo's restaurant."[29]

In contrast, the well-known Sambo's chain that launched in Santa Barbara repeatedly denied its origins in public forums. It ran advertising starting in 1961 in which a stereotyped image of a boy from India appeared as the logo, such as that for the grand opening of an outlet in Medford. Like Richard's Restaurant and Slave Market, Sambo's opened in locations that were sundown towns—Medford, Eugene, and Salem, Oregon; and Eureka, California. Or, they opened in towns with a significant Ku Klux Klan presence (e.g., Ukiah, California).[30] According to a journalist reporting that Medford's ignominious history was a thing of the past, the town had suffered a "minor flap" when a Black meteorologist was appointed to the town by the U.S. Weather Bureau. The opinion piece recounted that the meteorologist's (his name was not mentioned) presence had elicited "some arm-waving,

28. "Sambo Turns White," *Statesman Journal*, August 15, 1966, https://www.newspapers.com/image/198820501 (accessed October 12, 2017).

29. "Coast Group Plans Events," *The Capital Journal*, October 18, 1966, https://www.newspapers.com/image/316198532 (accessed October 12, 2017).

30. Loewen, *Sundown Towns*; "A Largely Attended Meeting of the Ku Klux Klan Was Held at Santa Rosa Friday Night. A Klan was Organized at Ukiah Earlier in the Week," *Petaluma Argus-Courier*, December 15, 1924, https://www.newspapers.com/image/222916779 (accessed November 4, 2017); Loewen, "Sundown Towns." http://sundown.tougaloo.edu/sundowntowns.php. (accessed November 27, 2017).

some tut-tutting and a bit of vicious rumor-mongering."[31] In fact, the family had suffered a cross burning on their lawn, and left thereafter.[32] Yet, the *Medford Times* reported that he had simply been promoted and assigned elsewhere, that humanity had prevailed among the residents, "and that was that." In this telling, Medford had indeed once been a sundown town, but the reputation was no longer deserved, because "a dark face no longer creates a sensation," particularly traveling entertainers.[33]

But Medford was undoubtedly a sundown town, a fact widely known in the region. The town's Human Rights Council admitted in 1963 that, in the past, "Negroes and other racial minorities were definitely not welcome here. In some cases of record, many years ago, police officers were assigned to see that no such individuals were permitted to remain here overnight."[34] The Council concluded, however, that conditions were much improved, an assessment that was overly optimistic. In 1963, Medford retailers conspired to prevent a Black family from buying groceries, prompting them to move away after six months. And, as was true in other sundown towns, Klan rallies and gatherings demonstrated to Black people that their safety depended on White goodwill. In some cases, implicit messaging was not enough, and the Klan terrorized Black individuals, such as George Burr, a Medford bootblack. Klansmen hung him briefly from a tree, cut him down, and ordered him to leave town.[35]

---

31. "To Avoid Racial Problems," *Medford Mail Tribune*, May 9, 1962, http://www.newspapers.com/image/96795288 (accessed November 4, 2017).

32. Loewen, "Sundown Towns."

33. "To Avoid Racial Problems."

34. "Sundown' No More," *Medford Mail Tribune*, July 18, 1963, https://www.newspapers.com/image/96845127 (accessed November 4, 2017).

35. Loewen, *Sundown Towns*.

Sundown towns like Medford also made travel difficult. Black travelers relied on sources such as the *Green Book* to travel, and at least in some municipalities, when businesses refused them service, Black private homes were an option for shelter. No such possibility existed in sundown towns, and driving through them was a risky proposition. This was acute in Oregon—only one city (Portland) in the whole state appears in the 1954 *Green Book*.[36] Professor Allison Blakely recalled that his friend carried a loaded pistol on his passenger seat when he drove through Medford and other southwestern Oregon cities.[37]

It therefore speaks volumes that Sambo's executives chose to open a restaurant brand that carried a racial epithet as its name in a town that instilled racial terror in Black people. The Medford restaurant made explicit mention of Bannerman's story. For example, "Mama MUMBO'S Special" was advertised as a choice of juice, an egg, and four Sambo Cakes. And, despite the story's original setting in India, the advertisement hails the menu as serving "The finest pancakes west of the Congo." The same language about the Congo was present in a grand opening advertisement for a new location at 1675 Franklin in Eugene.[38] Not only was the restaurant founded squarely on *Little Black Sambo*, it supplemented the racial tropes already at the story's core with derogatory references to Africa.

Industry pundits also understood the genesis of the restaurant name to be the children's story. In commenting on the new

36. Victor Green, *The Negro Travelers' Green Book: The Guide to Travel and Vacations,* facsimile edition.(1954; Camarillo, Calif.: About Comics, 2017).

37. Loewen, *Sundown Towns.*

38. Classified advertisement, *Medford Mail Tribune,* April 21, 1961, https://www.newspapers.com/image/96657067 (accessed October 12, 2017); classified advertisement, *Eugene Guard*, October 3, 1962, https://www.newspapers.com/image/109298831 (accessed October 12, 2017).

wave of pancake restaurant franchises that were sweeping the nation, the editor of *Fast Food Magazine* wondered, "Where's Black Sambo?" He reminisced in a 1960 column about Little Black Sambo's "heroic pancake eating fest" and noted that his son was endlessly entertained by the book, wanting it read to him at least six times daily. The editor "always liked the Black Sambo diet" and found the pancake craze to be one with significant potential.[39]

The Eureka restaurant found footing with families soon after its launch, and included oblique references to the Sambo story (e.g., "Six Sambo cakes, one fresh ranch egg, two strips of bacon, Tiger butter, and your choice of syrup").[40] When a new location was in the works for Salem, Oregon, the Sambo's theme was more explicitly racially marked. *The Statesman Journal* reported that "The Little Black Sambo restaurant chain is attempting to acquire property in Salem to build a restaurant and 100 living units." The restaurant would be in a block bounded by Commercial, Liberty, Mill, and Trade Streets SE. It is striking that this newspaper account repeated the name as the full title of Bannerman's book. Whether this was merely a colloquial usage volunteered by newspaper staff or the formal name filed by the restaurant management, it is important that the company allowed the story to run as such.[41] It opened on April 18, 1966, as the fifty-third outlet in the Sambo's chain, but, just two months

39. "Where's Black Sambo?," *Fast Food Magazine*, April 1960.

40. Classified advertisement, *Eureka Humboldt Standard*, January 27, 1962, https://www.newspapers.com/image/17544931 (accessed October 11, 2017); classified advertisement, *Eureka Humboldt Standard*, May 11, 1963, https://www.newspapers.com/image/17488155 (accessed October 11, 2017).

41. "Restaurant Chain Seeking Site," *Statesman Journal*, April 24, 1963, https://www.newspapers.com/image/80542755 (accessed October 12, 2017).

later, the restaurant ran into difficulty, with contractors filing a lien on the building at 480 Liberty Street SE for unpaid work.[42]

Sam Battistone Sr. was still president of the company, along with his partner F. Newell Bohnett, president of the Purchasing Corp. Battistone Jr. was manager of an outlet at 1025 South Riverside in Medford—he would go on to be elected president in 1967, with the founders becoming cochairmen.[43] Battistone Sr. and Bohnett oversaw the opening of additional outlets that all made liberal use of Bannerman's motifs, and about which no mention was made of the so called "Sam-bo" acronym. Coverage of new store openings (e.g., San Bernadino, California) said little about the chain's executives, Battistone and Bohnett, other than to state that they were the cofounders of restaurants in five states.[44]

But by 1969, when the restaurant made a public stock offering and began to expand rapidly, restaurant announcements now made specific reference to the origin of the chain's name.[45] When the brand came to Greeley, Colorado, one newspaper report claimed, "The name Sambo's is a contraction of the names of

42. "53rd Sambo Restaurant Opens Here," *The Capital Journal,* April 18, 1966, https://www.newspapers.com/image/316288226 (accessed October 12, 2017); "Foreclosure Asked for Cafe," *Statesman Journal,* https://www.newspapers.com/image/198228708 (accessed October 12, 2017).

43. *Medford Mail Tribune,* April 9, 1963, https://www.newspapers.com/image/96939769 (accessed October 12, 2017); "Men at the Top: Founder's Son Elected President of Sambo's," *Los Angeles Times,* October 2, 1967, https://www.newspapers.com/image/164798948 (accessed October 12, 2017).

44. "New Sambo's Restaurant to Open in S.B., *San Bernadino County Sun,* August 4, 1965, https://www.newspapers.com/image/55337877 (accessed October 11, 2017).

45. Robert Metz, "Market Place: Why Sambo's Is in Trouble," *New York Times,* November 27, 1981.

company co-founders, Sam Battistone Sr., and F. Newel Bohnett, who began the chain as a single restaurant in Santa Barbara in 1957." Notwithstanding that this etiology had never been mentioned in the fourteen years that the chain had been operating, it was now trotted out as historical fact. As well, the article downplayed the significance of the tiger, quoting Dick Roberts, the company's territorial director in saying that the "tiger butter" reflected "imaginative merchandising which is popular with children."[46]

Clearly, by this time, it had become tenuous to make explicit public linkages to the antiblackness on which the restaurant was founded. The owners now attempted to plead both innocence and ignorance. Not only had they named the chain after a contraction of their two names—by happenstance creating a racist epithet that dated to the country's earliest years—they only took on Bannerman's imagery after the fact, as a happy coincidence. Even if this explanation were credible, the owners had not articulated why they sought to attach the restaurant to a story that was unflinching in its depiction of Black debasement. They had also failed to explain how these men, born in 1914 and 1924, would have been oblivious to the tale at a time when it was wildly popular across the nation. Critically, legal documents show that the founders were not only aware of the story but explicitly referenced it in recounting the restaurant's launch. In a major lawsuit, the restaurant's counsel declared that Battistone's son, a child at the time, had conjured the chain's name. He "suggested the name 'Sambo's' as an appropriate title for a pancake house restaurant. The name was suggested because given Bannerman's

46. "Sambo's Restaurant Chain Plans Greely Operation," *The Greely Daily Tribune*, September 24, 1969,

book, it conjured up associations with pancakes and, coincidentally, combined the names of the founders."[47]

Public Controversies

The switch in branding was no doubt due to the controversy and protest that the restaurant name, like its namesake book, began to attract. Russell Kirk, a commentator in the *Los Angeles Times*, wrote with contempt about the national pushback against Bannerman's book, calling it censorship. And, in a strange conflation, he asked sarcastically, "didn't you know that Little Black Sambo was a notorious racist?" making the character himself the racist. Kirk held that the opposition was humorless, engaged in zealotry that made it inappropriate to take notice of an individual's racial characteristics or to be aware of geographical and cultural facts from around the world. Referring to a school ban in New York City, the writer asked, "What's wrong with the little black fellow? Why, he's distinctly called black, you see, and that's discriminatory . . . Is it wicked for Little Black Sambo to be black? Well . . . allow me to inform you that most people who live in Indian jungles are black—mostly distinctly black of skin. I don't see anything wrong with this." Citing the book's author as an English woman and the story's setting in India, Kirk concluded that "not only is Little Black Sambo no American child—he isn't even an African Negro." Finally, Kirk argued that the story of triumph was likely to elicit quite the opposite reaction from White children than what protestors believed; the story would in fact persuade White children to *like* Black children. Indeed,

---

47. United States Court of Appeals, Sixth Circuit. 1981. Sambo's Restaurants, Inc., v. The City of Ann Arbor, 663 F.2d 686.

children adored his bravery and sartorial splendor, and "hug Little Black Sambo dolls to their bosoms."[48]

Gelastic Jones wrote in to the *Fresno Bee* to say that it was a surprise to find in a Sambo's restaurant that "the picture of Little Black Sambo was not black at all, but rather, golden color. I asked about why this was so and I was informed that pressure was put upon the restaurant. At one time the decor was a truly black Sambo, but this was supposed to have been degrading. It seems like this is destroying our American childhood stories unnecessarily."[49] Jones's comments echoed those of many other Whites, for whom the tradition of racism was heritage they were not willing to discard "unnecessarily." And in questioning whether a "truly black Sambo" was in fact degrading, Jones asserts that majoritarian pleasures in the book ought to set the frame for how to interpret it. This was the stance the restaurant management took. Sambo's continued to shrug innocently, and other issues began unraveling the brand's position.

Once a Wall Street favorite, Sambo's began to falter in 1977. Earnings had been falling precipitously and the Securities and Exchange Commission was investigating the company's reporting practices. At issue was the incentive program for managers. These employees received low basic salaries of $9,000 per year but were able to participate in a complicated incentive program called "Fraction of the Action." After paying $20,000 for a 20 percent share of their profits, managers could also buy shares in other restaurants. Some managers benefitted tremendously from this program, but this was only possible when the chain was

48. Russell Kirk, "The Victim—Little Black Sambo." *The Los Angeles Times*, November 5, 1964, https://www.newspapers.com/image/165955451 (accessed October 12, 2017).

49. "Awfully Juvenile," *The Fresno Bee*, September 23, 1973, https://www.newspapers.com/image/25767137 (accessed October 12, 2017).

expanding. It was essentially a pyramid scheme. The SEC challenged the fact that corporate was treating the $20,000 payment as income rather than a deposit, and the company had to revise downward its earnings trajectory for the next twenty years and change the incentive program. The new program was rejected by managers, resulting in lawsuits and defections. Market analysts saw the abrupt end of the incentive program as the company's fatal error. Without the program, managerial staff would not continue working long hours without days off, which had fueled the company's profitability. One manager, charging that the incentive program was fraudulent, was awarded $925,000 in a lawsuit. Moreover, Sambo's had to buy back the shares of managers who left, further straining its liquidity, dampening earnings, and increasing debt. Shareholders began to revolt and nearly elected dissidents to the company's board. Amid this turmoil, Sambo's was also embroiled in litigation over its name: "Although the company says the story has nothing to do with its name, the chain's symbol is a tiger, a central character in the story."[50]

In 1979, Sam D. Battistone (the junior Battistone) was replaced as president and CEO. The restaurant had been in trouble financially for some time and had been pressured by its lenders to replace the company's management. Battistone was moved to chairman, leaving CEO vacant, and Karl V. Willig moved from executive vice president to president. The company lost $2.9 million in the first quarter of the year, compared to a profit of $3 million over the same period a year earlier. As well, losses were forecast for the remainder of 1979. Battistone blamed the SEC's ruling, arguing that it resulted in enormous manage-

50. Metz, "Market Place"; Pamela, G. Hollie, "A New Shake at Sambo's: Motel 6 Team Seeks to Turn Chain Around," *New York Times, December 3, 1979*; "Sambo's Must Pay Ex-employee $925,000 over Charge of Fraud," *Wall Street Journal*, July 21, 1981.

ment turnover and an inability to find qualified replacements. Inexperienced newcomers were further exacerbating declines in per-store earnings.[51] But shortly after these in-house changes, Sambo's took up a new management team, imported wholesale from officers at the hotel chain Motel 6. The challenges for the new leadership were described as "squabbles over the name and mass defections of restaurant operators."

As the company's finances foundered, the name "squabbles" picked up steam. Protests were erupting in cities where Sambo's sought to open. In Hartford, the State Commission on Human Rights and Opportunities asked the restaurant to change its name. In Brockton, Massachusetts, a mill city south of Boston, the License Commission withheld the restaurant's license until it could determine whether it could order the chain to change its name. Other towns on Cape Cod and elsewhere on mainland Massachusetts were also investigating their options, and as the U.S. District Court in Massachusetts considered a ban on the name, the attorney general's office argued that "the name 'Sambo' is understood by numerous residents of the Commonwealth of Massachusetts as offensive and demeaning to black people. It is understood as a badge of slavery and as a racial epithet." Newspapers were often equivocal on this point—syndicated news coverage reported, "'Sambo' is offensive, the opponents say, because the word was once an insulting nickname for black people."[52]

In Ithaca, the Black Caucus sought an injunction against the

51. Metz, "Market Place"; "Sambo's Replaces Battistone as Chief," *The Journal Times,* July 12, 1979, https://www.newspapers.com/image/343585658 (accessed November 4, 2017).

52. "Sambo's Asked to Change Name," *The Baltimore Afro-American,* September 30, 1978; 1978. "Children's Story Trips Up Restaurant Chain," *Ironwood Daily Globe,* August 9, 1978; "What's in Sambo's Name?" *Annapolis Capital,* September 27, 1978.

restaurant's signage under the premise that it would be a barrier to minority customers and was therefore discriminatory. At that time, the company had already withstood six other lawsuits in other jurisdictions.[53] Chain spokesman David Severson stated in 1978 that, despite having expanded all over the country, it was only in the Northeast that objections were raised, intimating that it was overly sensitive East Coast liberals who were responsible. In fact, as early as 1961, the NAACP had protested the Eureka outlet over the restaurant's sign. Controversy raged in Ithaca newspaper opinion pages. According to Clarice B. Abbott, the restaurant's challenges were tantamount to inflammatory race baiting concocted by Cornell's "ultra-liberals." Said Abbott, "The silent majority—it seems to me—is getting tired of being pushed around by the minorities and their self-appointed advocates." Other residents, such as Gould P. Colman, were opposed: "I know, and lots of other people know, that the word Sambo is equivalent to nigger. We also know it is indecent to put up signs . . . even when the sign is justified by the desire to make money. Shame on you, Sambo's Inc. May our paths never cross."[54]

Editorials also appeared in the Black press and leading national newspapers. "The owners tried to palm off this atrocious insult by alleging ingenuously that the name had nothing to do

53. Ted Walsh, "Sambo's Sign under Attack," *Syracuse Post Standard,* September 1, 1979.
54. 1978. "Tiger's Tale Gives Restaurant Chain a Bad Name," *The Ithaca Journal*, August 10, 1978, https://www.newspapers.com/image/255142380 (accessed October 12, 2017); *Eureka Humboldt Standard*, November 7, 1961, https://www.newspapers.com/image/25712861 (accessed October 12, 2017); 1979. "Sambo's Issue Conceived by Cornell 'Ultra-Liberals,'" *The Ithaca Journal*, November 14, 1979, (accessed October 12, 2017); "Shame on You, Sambo's," *The Ithaca Journal,* October 25, 1979, https://www.newspapers.com/image/255148178 (accessed October 12, 2017).

with the 'Little Black Sambo' of historical infamy but was merely an artful combination of their names," said Gerald Horne in the *Amsterdam News*.[55] In an editorial that ran in the *Washington Post* and other papers, William Raspberry questioned whether "Sam Battistone is putting you on when he tells you he doesn't understand the flap over Sambo's, the name of the restaurant chain he heads."[56] Raspberry noted that Battistone's protestations in all innocence over the origin of the name, and the company's stance that offense was taken only by a small subset of oversensitive individuals were not credible.

Sambo's sued the City of Ann Arbor, Michigan, in 1980 in the U.S. Court of Appeals, Sixth Circuit. When, in 1971, the chain sought to open in the town, the City Council balked at the name. Sambo's agreed to change it, and employed "Jolly Tiger" instead. After doing business as such for six years, it applied to change the name back to Sambo's. The permits were granted but revoked after the signs were erected, citing contravention of the prior agreement. Sambo's refused to take them down, and Ann Arbor threatened to sue. Sambo's then filed suit seeking "declaratory and injunctive relief for violations of its constitutional rights"; that is, to prevent the city from taking any action to restrict or prohibit its use of the name. The opinion was written by Judge Celebrezze, with Merritt concurring, and ruled in favor of Sambo's.[57]

Ann Arbor claimed that Sambo's had waived its First Amendment rights in originally agreeing to change the name and the district court had agreed. But the appeals court held that in

55. Gerald Horne, "Boycott as a Weapon, a Lesson of Sambo's," *The Amsterdam News*, January 2, 1982.
56. William Raspberry, "'Sambo's: Is There No Shame in the Name?" *The Washington Post*, November 14, 1977.
57. United States Court of Appeals, Sixth Circuit. 1981. Sambo's Restaurants, Inc., v. The City of Ann Arbor, 663 F.2d 686.

fact Sambo's could not have asserted those rights in 1972, as the Supreme Court did not grant commercial speech protection until 1976. The court also held that "we must also reject the proposition that otherwise protected commercial speech is stripped of that protection because of its ancillary offensiveness." Judge Merritt also opined that just as "our legal system does not permit a state or local school board to threaten the parents of black children with economic reprisals or boycotts in order to induce them to enter a contract foregoing their rights to the equal protection of the law," the same protections should hold for Sambo's. Celebrezze also argued that over the past twenty-four years, the company had invested substantial resources in the name Sambo's and that "substantial goodwill is attributed to that name, and it constitutes a valuable property interest." This argument is a clear articulation of what legal scholar Cheryl Harris theorizes about whiteness—that it acts as a kind of property right.[58] In this case, Sambo's financial investments in maintaining a racist name was a property interest that merited protection under the law.

With regard to the name being an epithet, the court held that both parties agreed that the name was not intended to be degrading, but that "certain citizens" might be offended and that it can be offensive to "some black people if directed at them," though other Black people "are not so offended." Moreover, according to the court, the city had provided no tangible evidence that the restaurant name had disrupted racial harmony. Judge Keith dissented, with one of the primary arguments being that the facts as presented glossed over the offensiveness of the name. Published work had shown that Black children endured taunts from White counterparts, were called Black Sambo, and became the embodiment of the story in all-White classrooms, suffering through class

58. Cheryl I. Harris, "Whiteness as Property," *Harvard Law Review* 106, no. 8 (1993): 1707–91.

readings. "This offensiveness and harm is not lessened simply because the word is contained in an advertisement or placed on a sign 30 feet in the air." Citing hearings at the Rhode Island Human Rights Commission, Keith's dissenting opinion found that the name necessarily acted to discourage Black patronage and unequal access to public accommodations. The commission argued that the name notified Black persons that "their patronage was unwelcome, objectionable, and not acceptable, desired, or solicited." Keith's opinion held that Sambo's had every opportunity to present contrary evidence to refute this assertion but had not, and the commission's findings were therefore entitled to great weight.

In 1979, Sambo's was still advertising widely, even courting older adults in the lives of graduating high school students at Cantwell High School in Montebello, California. But by 1981, the

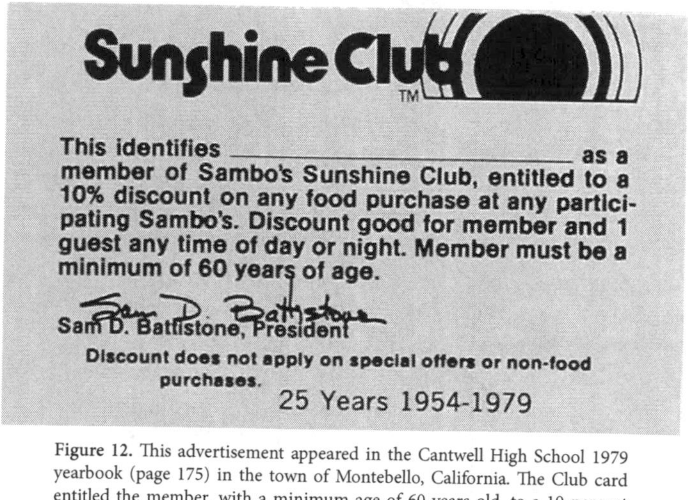

Figure 12. This advertisement appeared in the Cantwell High School 1979 yearbook (page 175) in the town of Montebello, California. The Club card entitled the member, with a minimum age of 60 years old, to a 10 percent discount on any food purchase at participating Sambo's. Source: ancestry.com, "Schools, Directories, & Church Histories."

restaurant chain was rumored to be on the verge of bankruptcy. Within the month of November alone, the restaurant closed 447 of the 1,114 restaurants it was operating; some restaurants were reportedly closed so abruptly that customers in the midst of their meals were hurried out so that the restaurant could be shut.[59] The closings were meant to stop the bleeding in lost patronage and profitability. But apart from dealing with lawsuits from former managers who lost out in the scuttling of the incentive scheme, the corporation was mired in litigation with itself. Sambo's sued former company executives Willig (president) and Wagner (executive VP and CEO) for defrauding the restaurant chain; they were indicted with mail and wire fraud and scheming to falsify cattle sale records involved in a kickback scheme. In addition to this $8 million suit, the company also sued former employees in response to their employees' having supported lawsuits against the company.[60]

Sambo's Today

The chain eventually succumbed to bankruptcy, and in an ironic twist, several of the chain's locations were bought by Denny's, another restaurant chain brand imbricated with racial discrimination—in the 1990s it faced class-action lawsuits for a raft of discriminatory practices ranging from requiring Black customers to prepay for meals to locking them out and barring their entry. In 1983 Denny's began acquiring Sambo's stores across

59. Metz, "Market Place: Why Sambo's Is in Trouble"; Horne, "Boycott as a Weapon."

60. Pamela, G. Hollie, "Sambo's Files More Lawsuits: Discord Looms at Its meeting," *New York Times*, June 26, 1980; "Two Ex-top Officials of Sambo's, 3 Others Are Indicted for Fraud," *Wall Street Journal,* November 25, 1981.

the country.[61] But one store—the original in Santa Barbara—remained open, despite losing its luster over time. In 1998, Chad Stevens, the grandson of Sam Battistone, sought to refurbish that location and relaunch a chain. It is unclear what has happened with the plans for a chain, but the outlet now serves what appears to be a large clientele. Santa Barbara's tourism site "Visit Santa Barbara" promotes the restaurant in a section advising travelers with children. A three-day itinerary for activities on the city's waterfront includes a visit Sambo's: "This is the 'ORIGINAL' Sambo's Restaurant that started it all! The restaurant is currently owned and managed by the original founders' grandson, Chad Stevens. (In fact SAMBO's name has it's roots based solely on the original "franchise" formed by Sam (Sam Battistone) and Bo—Sam's business associate, Newell Bohnett)." The tourism board took pains to head off any charge of racism by bringing the brand's sanitized etymology to the fore.

Remarkably, Hotel Milo, the site of the original (and current) Santa Barbara location makes no mention of the restaurant at all on its site, sanitized or not. Lindsey L. of Los Angeles pointed out on Yelp in April 2017 that "they don't advertise this but Sambo's restaurant is located on the hotel property and it's a good place to grab lunch since there's no room service." Indeed, the hotel fact sheet lists the following amenities: wifi, L'Occitane bath products, pools and jacuzzis, bicycles, a fitness center; minibar and in-room coffee, business services, and an oceanfront bistro serving local fruit and pastries. The only brief mention of Sambo's is buried in an archived blog post about Spring Break, where it is noted that "Hotel Milo also has an onsite diner named

61. "Denny's Remodeling Sambo's," *Daily Press*, March 2, 1983, https://www.newspapers.com/image/234100161 (accessed May 30, 2018).

Figure 13. A screenshot from the contemporary Sambo's website. Taken August 27, 2018.

Sambo's that's also a favorite early morning option."[62] This despite the fact that Sambo's is clearly valued by hotel patrons. For example, Jennifer K. of Thousand Oaks, California wrote in July 2012, "The complimentary breakfast buffett *[sic]* is mostly breads and cereal, but The Sambo Cafe is right on the property and is a great breakfast stop!"

When Stevens announced his plans in 1998, he reanimated the same debates about the name that took place decades earlier. Historian Robin Kelley was quoted as arguing that the image of Sambo "will always be linked to the stupid, shuffling black male. And no matter what they do, it will never be OK for a white man to operate a Sambo's." At that time, Stevens gave the same justification for the name that his forbears used, and attributed the controversy to the 1960s and 1970s being "a very sensitive time. There was a sense of political correctness and militancy."

---

62. "Spring Break 24 Hrs.," 2018. https://www.hotelmilosantabarbara.com/blog/santa-barbara-spring-break-24-hours/.

Still, he also claimed that, "If we get complaints about the name in the future, that's something we'll think about and deal with."[63]

Stevens had precisely that opportunity when Yelp reviewers began commenting on the racism inherent in the restaurant's name. His responses were confused. Even as he denied any racism, intended or otherwise, he acknowledged that the restaurant had used Bannerman's original story, a break from the founders' position. Indeed, the current website displays a menu featuring the same racist tropes as the midcentury outlets (e.g., Mama Mumbo and Papa Jumbo entrées). Trailing off in digressions and non sequiturs, he asserted that the meaning of Sambo was essentially in the eyes of the beholder. As seen in the quotes below, his speech was marred by the kinds of linguistic incoherence that characterizes White discourse about racism:[64]

Dear C.O.C. I first want to thank you for your post and I understand your feeling about the negative conitations associated with the name Sambo. But when using this name for my family restaurant it was a combination of my grandfathers name (Sam) and his partner (Bo). They used a story about a boy from India that lost his clothes to some tigers. The tigers ran around a tree and turned into butter and is Mother made him Pancakes. This boys name was Sambo, and it was never ment to be used in a negative way. I am sorry that some people still feel this way about the word Sambo. When we use the name Sambo at the restaurant it is used in a positive manner, I hope you can understand the legacy of a great restaurant chain my grandfather and his partner created. On a side note did you know the Vice President of Nigerea is named Sambo? Thank you once again and if you would like we

63. Valerie Burgher, "Sambo's Owner Plans Comeback for Eatery," *Los Angeles Times*, January 12, 1998, https://www.newspapers.com/image/160089821 (accessed November 4, 2017).

64. Eduardo Bonilla-Silva, *Racism without Racists: Color-Blind Racism and the Persistence of Racial Inequality in the United States,* 2nd ed. (New York: Rowman & Littlefield, 2006).

could talk in more detail. I am open to learning and understanding different points of view. Chad (9/11/2012)

Juliana, I am unsure if you know that the name Sambos has many meanings. The former Vice President of Nigeria in 2014 name is Namadi Sambo, should he change his name. Also the word Sambo is a type of wrestling based on Judo. The way we use Sambo is its about an Indian Child from a popular book "Little Black Sambo," which is a top selling book in Japan. I do not support anything raciest and despise anyone or group that supports raciest thoughts. I am proud of what my grandfather created almost 70 years ago and I hope that the good thoughts about the name carry on. I agree that the bad thoughts and using the name in a negative connotation should stop. Thank you for your views. (8/11/2015)

However, using the search tool on Yelp's website reveals that few of the more than six hundred reviews make any mention of racism.[65] Of these, some made hesitant commentary about the possibility of the branding being racist but reported enjoying their meals and the establishment nonetheless; others dismissed the charges altogether. A reviewer on TripAdvisor, TravelingIguana from Newtown, Massachusetts, wrote on November 12, 2017, "Right next door from morning through lunch is the unfortunately named "Sambo's" (really? can't you change the name in 2017? So racist.)."

Other internet forums decried accusations of racism as political correctness. Perceiving the original restaurant's demise to be the fault of militant and deluded Black agitators, they railed against the stifling "PC" tenor of public discourse, particularly about something so innocent as a restaurant. Sambo's was remembered fondly by many, who wrote about the positive experiences they had in the restaurant, something that was unfairly denied others upon its closing. For example, at the website "Old

65. "Yelp: Sambo's Restaurant," 2017 https://www.yelp.com/biz/sambos-restaurant-santa-barbara.

L.A. Restaurants," the site's author stated that a colleague once remarked "that the only tragedy of the civil rights movement of the sixties was in the demise of Sambo's Restaurants." As Chad Stevens contended, the Civil Rights movement is cast here as essentially a protracted exercise in political correctness. The author asserted that the term Sambo only came to denote an "ugly racial image" years after the restaurant launched in 1957, and that the chain simply could not make enough modifications to satisfy opponents. One hundred and thirty-seven comments such as the below came in to the post:

> This PC junk is out of hand! We went to the one on 6th and Vermont in Los Angeles as teenagers in the early 70s. We were a wild bunch, and we never associated the place with anything racial, and believe me we would have if there was a way. (Robert, February 13, 2017, 8:11 am).

> I miss Sambo's! So tired of the PC left. My best memory of Sambo's was going there after Grad nite in 79 with my date, pancakes and coffee as the sun came up. (Carol, December 4, 2016, 10:31 am).

> I wish for those simpler times without the word smithing that goes into everything these days. (Mark Ryan, July 27, 2016, 12:02 pm)

> The people who had an ax to grind with 'Sambo's' did nothing but destroy a restaurant chain, put thousands of people out of work, and accomplish absolutely nothing in the name of civil rights. (Chuck Parmenter, March 28, 2016, 9:54 am)

> Remember as a 10yr old kid the political and black community railing against the local coffee shop. I couldn't see their point. That was the beginnings of reverse discrimination, blacks muckraking, and its only gotten more rediculous since then. At 10 it was apparent a black movement was out to get revenge by destroying an innocent restaurant because of a name and characature. Their way to lash back but good people got hurt. (Mike L., August 8, 2015, 8:29 pm)

How tragic that the stupidity of political correctness killed off a well loved restaurant chain. Just ridiculous. Believe it or not one of my favorite stories as a kid in the '60s was Little Black Sambo. At that time it had no offensive connotations and never occurred to me. If anything it was a good reference. (Jeff Brodbeck, October 22, 2014, 9:39 pm)

Some Restaurants did have a black (not Indian Boy). It's nothing to be ashamed of. It is sad that so many ignorant People targeted Sambo's as racist. (James, April 2, 2014, 6:18 am)

Wow. My father actually bought Sambo's stock. We watched it go down in flames. I was pre adolescent, so I was unaware of the lawsuit and racial terrorism inflicted on the owners. Shame, shame. People seem to judge on such limited information, never having all the facts. And who are we to judge, anyway? (Jennifer, July 27, 2013, 1:33 pm)

Conclusion: The Spice of Racism

ALL FOUR RESTAURANTS suggest that racism makes food taste better. Racism lends an added spice to restaurant dining ranging from relatively tony full-service establishments to roadhouse eateries and fast casual chains. Across quite different settings, these restaurants have made antiblackness their central premise. Because racism is the way American society does business, the establishments reviewed here may at first blush suggest simply another—if unique—example of how that business is done. But it is meaningful that these outlets are restaurants and not bookstores, auto supply shops, or hotels. What is it about the combination of racism and the provision of meals that makes these businesses a draw?

Certainly, nostalgia for a past in which Black people were relegated to servitude has traction in many public arenas, including literature, film, and television. And racial caricatures of Black people in subservient positions grace the packaging of manifold products. Racist restaurants, like these products, may evoke nostalgia for slavery itself, and the racial dictatorship it comprised.[1] It is also possible that racist restaurants mobilize

1. Omi and Winant, *Racial Formation in the United States.*

the culture, geography, and institutions of the South. They pay tribute to social structures in which mobility was severely constrained for Black Americans and constitute simple reminders of the wages of Whiteness.

Images of faithful slaves have arisen in reaction to eras in which Black folk have pressed for racial equality, and for that reason it could be expected to find Mammy a popular image in the 1950s and 1960s as the Civil Rights movement ignited radical social change.[2] Along those lines, Sambo's and Richard's came into being in the 1950s.

But beyond that, if White patrons enjoy dining in settings where their racial superiority is explicit, and those same pleasures are not extended to other retail and consumer contexts, other processes must be at work. The racial work these restaurants do echoes the distinct concerns of differing schools of CRT thought: they affect and are affected by systems of images, discourse, and unconscious feelings; they allocate privilege and tangible benefits; and they advance variable racial projects that ebb and flow with prevailing social conditions.[3]

Capitalism always requires novelty and difference for products to stand out in a crowded marketplace, the more exotic and outré the better. Blackness is easy shorthand for exotic, and dehumanizing Black people makes them easily convertible into gimmick. The exoticism of bblackness therefore brings material benefits to those who use racism as a marketing tool. Objectified blackness makes these restaurants innovative and brings with it the added benefit of bringing diners that much closer to the earth, whence the food came or over which it was slaughtered and cooked. Blackness makes the food more

2. McElya, *Clinging to Mammy*.
3. Delgado and Stefanic, *Critical Race Theory*.

primal, subversive, and real. As noted earlier, cooking and serving food have been seen as intrinsic to Black women, and these restaurants offered meals thought to embody the culinary repertoire of Black people. It is for that reason that the Coon Chicken Inn was a phenomenon, rather than a Coon Auto Parts. Black people are thought to be naturally affiliated with food, and that connection creates a selling point for a restaurant; to connect coons with cars would not only be insensible, it would be a liability that would stain the business with a badge of inferior products, service, or implied customer base.

And yet there are competing forces in how blackness is constructed in relation to food. On the one hand, these restaurants provide satiation from a satisfying, often "authentic" meal, and satiation from the pleasurable reaffirmations of Black inferiority. On the other hand, two of the restaurants are people buildings, in which patrons are invited into the dining room through the Black body. In order to consume Black food, or food prepared by Blacks, or food prepared as though by Blacks, one has to be consumed by the Black body and therefore risk being destroyed. To eat is to be potentially destroyed; it is like preparing ackee or fugu when you don't know what you're doing. But perhaps by going inside the Black body, the White diner destroys it, much as Neo destroys Agent Smith by diving inside him—or at least appears to destroy Smith, before *Matrix Revolutions* shows him to be altered rather than dead. Might then these restaurants set up the potential for the duality of being able to destroy the despised Black body at the same time as being fed? Or to express contempt for the servant who is metaphorically providing the food, by literally wiping one's feet on him or her?

Either way, the racial caricature people buildings make objects out of Black people. Historically, there have been many restaurants shaped like the food they sell. Termed mimetic architecture, or logo buildings,[4] these structures that resemble the goods or services available at the establishment were particularly popular for restaurants and retail food outlets, especially during the 1940s and 1950s. Examples include a Long Island poultry stand in the shape of a duck, Mexican restaurants taking the shape of giant tamales, and fast food symbolized in giant root beer kegs.[5] But all of these buildings are objects, not people. Even those restaurant chains that employ people as logos and signposts, (e.g., Bob's Big Boy and Colonel Sanders) restrict them to signage and rooftops alone. Never do patrons walk inside these bodies. The racial order of racist restaurants transformed the coon and mammy into the realm of nonhuman object. The Black body, then, "principally holds value in its ability to entertain. Its humanity, culture, history, and dignity are erased and its voice is silenced."[6]

It is also true that the restaurants may loosen bodily boundaries, without total destruction. For example, in the case of Mammy's Cupboard, White consumers can tame the perceived unruliness of Black women's bodies and perceived excessiveness in relation to food. As Sabina Strings argues, "The discourse of obese black women engaging in behaviors that place themselves and others at risk is not solely, or principally, a matter of the (inconsistent) medical findings as they relate to weight and health. Instead, they are the latest innovation in the familiar medical trope of the unrestrained black women as

4. Dolores Hayden and Jim Wark, *A Field Guide to Sprawl* (New York: W. W. Norton, 2004).

5. Webb, "Tracking the Elusive 'Look at Me!' Buildings."

6. Sacha Hilhorst and Joke Hermes, "'We Have Given Up So Much': Passion and Denial in the Dutch Zwarte Piet (Black Pete) Controversy," *European Journal of Cultural Studies* 19, no. 3 (2016): 218–33 at 278.

deadly."[7] Strings contends that though there is abundant discourse about the idea of Black insatiability, one aspect of that, which has been little examined, is the notion of "unfettered indulgence in oral appetites." This notion is evident in historical texts such as racial encyclopedias, where African gluttony was a central construct.[8] By walking into a Black body, the White diner is able to partake of that gluttony and inhabit a perilous yet satisfying space where food can be consumed without the constraints of social decency. If Black bodies are thought to be animalistic and irrational, eating inside of them suggests a meal where the dictates of moral fitness may be tossed to the winds.

But these are rather metaphorical interpretations of why racism makes food taste better. There are more concrete explanations as well. Sambo's and Richard's Slave Market used names founded on the degradation of blackness and also located their restaurants in social spaces that were inhospitable and dangerous to Black people, thereby excluding them as patrons. In that regard, racist restaurants recreate/recover Jim Crow spaces. Like swimming pools, eating establishments were one of the most contested public spaces undergoing desegregation. White people were disgusted at having to eat with Black neighbors; although Black people were fit to prepare the food, dining with them was intolerable. The intimacy of eating was discordant with transracial spaces, and a vast body of memoirs by White authors shows that eating with Black people was "unthinkable."[9] If naming a restaurant Coon Chicken Inn or Mammy's Cupboard will not keep Black clientele away,

7. Sabrina Strings, "Obese Black Women as 'Social Dead Weight': Reinventing the 'Diseased Black Woman,'" *Signs: Journal of Women in Culture and Society* 41, no. 1 (2015):107–30 at 108.

8. Strings, "Obese Black Women as 'Social Dead Weight.'"

9. Cooley, *To Live and Dine in Dixie*, 5.

then buildings that brandish racial caricature probably will. The concrete explanation, simply put, is that these restaurants guarantee Whites-only spaces in public accommodations that should otherwise be open to all.

A second more concrete draw of racist restaurants is the spectacle. In a qualitatively different way, to be sure, but in the manner that lynchings invited a crowd, these restaurants make a very public display of racism, a display to buttress the country's racial hierarchies and the topmost position of whiteness within it. Customers who patronize these restaurants can share in the consumption of Black domination with others. Moreover, precisely because it is a less virulent display than the public spectacles of old, White consumers can indulge racist postures under the guise of kitsch, tradition, and Americana, and even chide for exceptional sensitivity those who would be offended. Indeed, while it may not have been the purpose of setting up these restaurants, their existence clearly allows Whites to buy into the idea that racism is gone, if it ever existed. Eating out at a restaurant is purely for pleasure, and restaurants named after racist epithets insist on their innocence by virtue of the goods they sell. It's Sambo's pancakes, after all, not Sambo's Police Brutality Gun Shop. As well, the racist caricatures that these restaurants employed are seen by Whites as simple, innocent, humorous, and even beloved. These outlets parse out "real racism" as expressions or depictions of maniacal animus; stereotypes that merely dehumanize Black people are not seen as racist if they elicit smiles.

The international scale of investments in racist imagery is useful as a comparative framework for the "willful" or "smug ignorance" over what can be described as an "unadulterated colonialism and racism."[10] British adults continue to profess fond-

10. Hilhorst and Hermes, "'We Have Given Up So Much'"; Yvon van der Pijl and Karina Goulordava, "Black Pete, 'Smug Ignorance,' and

ness for racist Golliwogs, and in the 1960s thought it "absurd to imagine that they could ever engender hostile feelings about race."[11] Scholars have argued that because Zwarte Piet ("Black Pete"), a racial caricature in blackface that is part of Christmas celebrations in the Netherlands, is directed at children, it is thought to be unassailably innocent. A commonly voiced viewpoint is that Black Pete itself is not racist, but "If you talk about it this way, you make it a problem and make it racist," said one high school student.[12] Similarly, statements about the racism inherent in Black Pete are often met with assertions that the person who believes so is deranged and absurd. When the leaders of the right-wing populist group Leefbaar Rotterdam attached Black golliwog-like dolls to lampposts and trees, the public denounced the action as mimicking lynchings. The group responded that these statements were "ridiculous and disgusting" and that "if you have these associations, you should go see a psychiatrist." This stance suggests that being unable to recognize racism is not a flaw but rather a mark of purity.[13] To call out racism is disgusting, not the racism itself.

The Zwarte Piet case is instructive in reading racist restaurants because it involves a public display of racism that is constructed as innocent tradition, and invites ignorance of deeply ingrained cultural messages and colonial histories. Indeed, discourse around Zwarte Piet often devolves into false analogies, that if Zwarte Piet is racism, then so is X and Y and Z, none of which have to do with racism (e.g., "Perhaps we shouldn't

---

the Value of the Black Body in Postcolonial Netherlands," *New West Indian Guide* 88 (2014): 262–91.

11. Lelyveld, "Now Little White Squibba Joins Sambo in Facing Jungle Perils."

12. Hilhorst and Hermes, "'We Have Given Up So Much,'" 283.

13. Hilhorst and Hermes, "'We Have Given Up So Much.'"

build snowmen, this is racism against Whites). Such discourse intimates "not just an inability to make out what is and is not racist; it is to glorify such an inability."[14] The same kinds of false equivalencies pervade discourse about racist restaurants, and the tenor of the discourse is similarly and surprisingly fraught with emotion. Just as contestations surrounding Zwarte Piet elicits acute anger, anxiety, hurt, and other strong feelings—passion— among "pro-Pieten,"[15] challenges to racist restaurants seem to enrage many average White Americans. Why should this be? What stake do they hold in the name or branding of restaurants with which they are not affiliated? In the case of Zwarte Piet, Dutch supporters argue that the country as a whole risks losing a longstanding cultural tradition and that, more specifically, Dutch (implied White) children face the hurt of losing special holiday festivities. Ignored is the possibility that Black Dutch children will be hurt by maintaining the celebration. Were proponents of Zwarte Piet to recognize this hurt, and therefore the fact that everyone feels a full spectrum of emotions, it would allow the nation to "settle on a form of courteousness; a courtesy not based on the suppression or hiding of animosity, but upon the acceptance that others, too, are fully human and capable of hurt."[16]

Is America ready for a similar reckoning?

14. Hilhorst and Hermes, "'We Have Given Up So Much,'" 224.
15. Hilhorst and Hermes, "'We Have Given Up So Much.'"
16. Hilhorst and Hermes, "'We Have Given Up So Much,'" 230.

Acknowledgments

The research conducted for this book and writing of the manuscript was supported by the National Library of Medicine of the National Institutes of Health under Award Number G13LM012463 (content is solely the responsibility of the author and does not necessarily represent the official views of the National Institutes of Health); a Senior Fellowship at the Smithsonian Institution's National Museum of American History; a Fellowship at the Black Metropolis Research Consortium, University of Chicago; and a fellowship from EURIAS at the Institute for Advanced Studies, Marseille, France, cofunded by Marie Sklodowska-Curie Actions, under the 7th Framework Programme.

Naa Oyo A. Kwate is associate professor of human ecology and Africana studies at Rutgers, The State University of New Jersey.